Vegan Boards

KATE KASBEE

Vegan Boards

50 Gorgeous Plant-Based Snack, Meal, and Dessert Boards for All Occasions

HARVARD
COMMON
PRESS

Inspiring | Educating | Creating | Entertaining

Brimming with creative inspiration, how-to projects, and useful information to enrich your everyday life, Quarto Knows is a favorite destination for those pursuing their interests and passions. Visit our site and dig deeper with our books into your area of interest: Quarto Creates, Quarto Cooks, Quarto Homes, Quarto Lives, Quarto Drives, Quarto Explores, Quarto Gifts, or Quarto Kids.

The Harvard Common Press titles are also available at discount for retail, wholesale, promotional, and bulk purchase. For details, contact the Special Sales Manager by email at specialsales@quarto.com or by mail at The Quarto Group, Attn: Special Sales Manager, 100 Cummings Center, Suite 265-D, Beverly, MA 01915, USA.

25 24 23 22 21   1 2 3 4 5

ISBN: 978-0-7603-7051-3

Digital edition published in 2021

Library of Congress Cataloging-in-Publication Data available

Design: Kelley Galbreath
Cover Image: Kate Kasbee
Page Layout: Kelley Galbreath
Photography: Kate Kasbee

Printed in China

For Andrew

Thank you for encouraging me,
taste-testing every recipe in
this cookbook, and taking my
kitchen messes in stride.

Contents

Inntroduction: A Beautiful Way
to Share Food | **9**

The Boards

CHAPTER 1 | 19
Breakfast and Brunch Boards

CHAPTER 2 | 37
Grazing at Home Boards

CHAPTER 3 | 69
Meal Boards

CHAPTER 4 | 91
Seasonal and Celebration Boards

CHAPTER 5 | 111
Fruit and Dessert Boards

The Recipes

128

Acknowledgments | **152**
About the Author | **153**
Index | **154**

A Beautiful Way to Share Food

I believe the greatest memories are made gathered around food and in between bites.

WHEN I WAS GROWING UP in Illinois, my parents had a sprawling strawberry patch behind the pool in our backyard. We grew other fruits and vegetables, too. Our garden heaved with produce each hot, humid summer. But I remember the strawberries more than anything else. They were unbelievably sweet and juicy and unlike anything I had ever tasted. To this day, strawberries remind me of home and of the Midwest, the place I fell in love with food.

I had a healthy relationship with food from a young age; I can thank my parents for that. We were the type of family that ate dinner together every night. In a somewhat unusual role reversal for the '90s, my dad was the main chef in our house. When he traveled for work, my mom had a small repertoire of dishes she could pull out of her back pocket to make sure my sister and I sat down for a home-cooked meal—even if it was meatloaf.

When my dad was in charge of the menu, there was no shortage of carbs on the table. It wasn't unusual for our family to devour a casserole dish of baked macaroni and cheese and a loaf of French bread with butter. I absolutely loved it. Pushing carbs on people was a practice I emulated as soon as I was old enough to cook and bake on my own. In fifth grade, I earned the nickname "Betty Crocker" among my classmates for bringing a themed cake to school each week.

I will never forget the surprise and delight on my friends' and teachers' faces the first time I arrived at school carefully balancing a cake on top of my notebooks and papers—and the second, third, and fourth times. At ten years old, it was my first taste of the joy that comes from sharing food with others. I was completely hooked.

Today, I still use food as a way to express my love and appreciation for the people I care about. You probably won't find me baking a cake from a box, though. Over the years, my food philosophy has shifted toward eating and sharing homemade, plant-based foods. One of my favorite ways to connect with others over food is through building grazing and family-style meal boards full of interesting colors, flavors, and textures that encourage interaction and exploration.

Except for strawberries, which you'll find on many boards in this cookbook, these aren't the foods I was raised on. Rather, they are the foods and flavors I've come to love through my curiosity, travels, and trying "just a bite" of everyone else's meal. They include fruits, vegetables, whole grains, and lots of fresh herbs, which add visual interest and a lovely aroma to each board.

Many of the breakfast and brunch, grazing, meal, and dessert boards in this cookbook celebrate whole foods. However, I haven't excluded packaged foods completely. Several recipes call

for tempeh, a fermented soy product that slices and crumbles beautifully, creating a satisfying meat substitute. You can try it on the Midsummer Backyard BBQ Board (page 95) and the Cincinnati-Style Chili Dinner Board (page 78).

You will occasionally see suggestions for vegan cheese products and packaged goods, like premade pie crust and pizza dough. Feel free to make these components from scratch. My goal in creating this book was to strike a balance of healthy recipes made with love and convenient foods that can be unwrapped and served in minutes. The wonderful thing about grazing and family-style meal boards is that you can use them as templates and tweak them to fit your own food philosophy.

My hope for this cookbook is that you will feel inspired to get in the kitchen and make something memorable to celebrate the small, in-between moments with the people you love. Whether it's a successful farmers' market haul, a movie night at home, or a summer backyard barbecue, I believe the greatest memories are made at home and gathered around food.

Board Building Basics (and How to Use This Book)

Building the perfect board starts with letting go of the idea of building the perfect board. Yes, you read that right. Even if you follow my instructions carefully, your board may look a little bit different than mine. That's okay! In fact, I hope your board doesn't look exactly like my board. While I will share the basics of assembling a board and a few tips for success, you will find ways to add your own touches and build a board that's unique. Build your board in a way that feels authentic to you, and try not to panic if it doesn't look precisely how you envisioned it. Your guests will be so delighted with the final result no matter what.

When building a board, the first thing to do is to read through the components, the how-to, *and* the recipes on the board. The amount of time it takes to build a board will depend almost entirely on the complexity of the recipes. If a recipe is gluten-free, soy-free, or nut-free, it will be noted beneath the recipe title. Minimize stress by selecting a board you feel confident you can complete before your friends and family arrive. Ideally, you'll have a grazing board already set out when your event begins so you can relax and mingle with your guests.

Meal boards are a bit different. The meal boards in this book are intended to be served at the dinner table and enjoyed seated. You can invite your friends and family to help you prepare the board, or assign your guests specific recipes or board components to contribute potluck style. In this scenario, all that's left to do at dinnertime is assemble the board and eat.

Now that you've selected a board and have an understanding of what it will take to make it happen, it's time to start cooking. I recommend starting with any component that requires extended freezing, refrigeration, or marinating first. Next, I usually make the cooked recipes and keep any items that need to be served warm in a 200°F (100°C or gas mark ½) oven until it's time to eat. Foods that turn brown when exposed to air, like apples, pears, and bananas, should be sliced and placed on the board last. I like to toss sliced fruit with a little bit of lemon juice to slow down the oxidation process. This makes for a much more attractive and appetizing board.

Once you have prepared all of the board components, it's time to put it all together. I almost always begin by placing anything in a bowl on the board first, starting with the largest bowl and placing smaller bowls in its orbit. This anchors the board and makes it feel balanced right off the bat. Then add the rest of the components to the board, from largest to smallest. If it's appropriate for the theme of the board, tucking sprigs of fresh herbs throughout will give the board a polished look and enticing aroma.

It's a good idea to place ingredients or recipes intended to be eaten together next to one another on the board. If cucumber slices are meant to be dipped in hummus, give your guests that cue by fanning the cucumber around the hummus bowl. Or you can choose to place unlikely items that pair well together next to one another to encourage your guests to try new flavor combinations.

A Note on Packaged Foods

As I mentioned earlier, several of the boards in this book call for packaged food items. If you would rather make these components from scratch, more power to you! I included packaged foods on these boards for one reason: they're convenient. I designed the boards this way intentionally. Building your boards with a blend of homemade and packaged foods will save you hours in the kitchen so you can spend more time enjoying your company.

I could write an entire chapter on interpreting ingredient labels; it's amazing how much added sugar is hiding in seemingly innocuous foods like marinara sauce, ketchup, and barbecue sauce. My general rule when buying a packaged food item is to choose one with a short and simple list of ingredients. If there are ingredients listed that you can't pronounce, try to find an alternative. I really like the Primal Kitchen brand for sauces and condiments because they have no added sugar. Plus, if a product is vegan, gluten-free, or soy-free, it's clearly labeled as such.

What You'll Need

Ask any of my friends and they'll tell you I'm a pretty thrifty person. I rarely buy anything at full price and I always shop my own home to redecorate before I purchase something new. I apply this principle to board building, too. A gorgeous board has little to do with the actual piece of wood. The color and quality of the serving bowls you set on that piece of wood don't matter much either, though I'll admit I have a growing collection.

With vegan boards in particular, the vibrant fruits and vegetables and velvety dips and sauces do all the talking. It's my recommendation to focus your resources on finding the freshest, highest-quality ingredients available to build your boards. After all, the food and how you present it is what your guests will remember most.

With this in mind, I bet you already have a few things in your kitchen you can use to build your first board right now. A quarter sheet pan makes a perfect board in a pinch—I used it to build the Grilled Cheese and Roasted Tomato Soup Board (page 83). If you have a set of nesting prep bowls you cook with, these make terrific vessels for small snacks like nuts and pomegranate seeds. Even measuring cups can stand in for bowls. Shop your own kitchen before heading out

5. Fruit

2. Smaller bowls

3. Crackers

4. Veggies

1. Largest bowl

A gorgeous board has little to do with the actual piece of wood.

to the store—you might have more supplies than you think.

Speaking of supplies, there are a few particular items that will be helpful to have as you explore the boards in this book. You'll notice that I suggest a certain board size with each board idea, but you can use whatever you have and it'll turn out great. If you are planning to invest in some new serving pieces, I recommend the following:

1 small round board (14-inch [35 cm] diameter)
1 medium rectangular board (11 x 16 inches [28 x 40 cm])
1 large round board (20-inch [50 cm] diameter)
1 large rectangular board (14 x 27 inches [35 x 70 cm])
1 marble pastry slab (16 x 24 inches [40 x 60 cm])
1 large bowl (10- to 12-inch [25 to 30 cm] diameter)
2 medium bowls (6- to 8-inch [15 to 20 cm] diameter)
5 small bowls (4- to 5-inch [10 to 12.5 cm] diameter)
2 oven-safe ramekins (5 ounces [140 g] each)
3 mini bowls or ramekins (1 ounce [28 g] each)

4 medium mason jars or glasses (10 to 12 ounces [280 to 340 g] each)
1 small mason jar (4 ounces [112 g])
3 serving spoons
1 pair of salad tongs
10 condiment spoons

The following are nice to have but certainly not essential:

Linen napkins
Cocktail picks
Small forks and spoons
Large glass pitcher
2 (16-ounce [454 g]) glass carafes
8 appetizer plates (5- to 6-inch [12.5 to 15 cm] diameter)

My go-to places to buy boards, bowls, and serving pieces are Crate & Barrel, Cost Plus World Market, and Sur La Table. I have also found some great vintage pieces, such as forks, spoons, and cocktail picks, on Etsy. A few of the little wooden spoons and chopsticks featured in this book are travel souvenirs and gifts from friends. It's fun to hunt for these one-of-a-kind pieces, and they make great conversation starters.

CHAPTER 1

Breakfast and Brunch Boards

Chia Pudding
Parfait Board
20

Sweet and Savory
Toast Board
23

Breakfast in Bed
Board
24

Grab-and-Go
Oatmeal Board
26

Sweet and Spicy Melon
Sparkler Board
28

Vegan Breakfast
Burrito Board
30

Sweet Potato Breakfast
Bowls Board
32

Build-Your-Own
Bagel Sandwich Board
34

◄◄ Sweet and Spicy Melon Sparkler Board (page 28)

Chia Pudding Parfait Board

SERVES 4

Fills an 11 x 16-inch (28 x 40 cm) rectangular board

4 servings Orange Vanilla Chia Pudding (page 143)

½ cup (120 g) salted peanut butter or almond butter

1 cup (120 g) gluten-free granola

1 cup (150 g) roasted and salted pistachios

½ cup (120 ml) maple syrup

2 tablespoons (16 g) ground cinnamon

2 kiwi, peeled and sliced

8 ounces (227 g) strawberries

6 ounces (168 g) raspberries

6 ounces (168 g) blackberries

1 pint (300 g) blueberries

Few sprigs of fresh mint

If you've never tried chia pudding, you're in for a treat. While some find the goopy texture a bit shocking at first, chia pudding becomes palatable and downright delicious when topped with nut butter, fresh fruit, maple syrup, and crunchy granola. This Chia Pudding Parfait Board would make a refreshing summer breakfast or brunch and is both vegan and gluten-free. Swap in your group's preferred fruits and nuts or use whatever is in season. The orange-vanilla flavor of the chia pudding is subtle and versatile enough to pair with a variety of toppings.

1 Place the Orange Vanilla Chia Pudding cups in a zigzag line down the middle of your serving board.

2 Spoon the peanut butter or almond butter into a 4-ounce (112 g) mason jar or small bowl and place it toward the middle of the board.

3 Pour the granola and pistachios into equal-size bowls and place them in two corners of the board.

4 Pour the maple syrup into a mini bowl and place it near the center of the board. Garnish with a honey dipper or a small spoon for serving. Shake the cinnamon into a small bowl and set it near the maple syrup.

5 Fan the kiwi slices around the chia pudding at the top of the board and the chia pudding at the bottom of the board.

6 Slice the strawberries in half lengthwise and group them in clusters at the bottom, middle, and top of the board.

7 Mix the raspberries and blackberries together and cluster them near the strawberries. Fill in any gaps on the board with the blueberries and garnish with a few fresh mint sprigs.

Sweet and Savory Toast Board

SERVES 6

Fills a 20-inch (50 cm) round board

1 cup (240 g) Rustic
Peach Jam with Thyme
(page 132)

1 batch Smoky Roasted
Carrots (page 133)

½ cup (120 g) hummus

½ cup (120 g) almond
butter

¼ cup (60 g) flaky sea salt

¼ cup (30 g) everything
bagel seasoning

¼ cup (35 g) capers

¼ cup (60 ml) agave
nectar

6 slices sourdough bread,
toasted

1 orange, sliced

1 bunch red seedless
grapes

6 Easter egg radishes,
thinly sliced

1 avocado, peeled, pitted,
and sliced

1 cup (30 g) microgreens

1 kiwi, cut in half

1 cucumber, peeled into
ribbons

1 pint (300 g) blackberries

1 bunch fresh dill

The savory/sweet debate is one I have with myself every morning as I think about what to eat for breakfast. This Sweet and Savory Toast Board simplifies the decision and offers something for everyone. I prefer sourdough toast as the vessel for my favorite toppings, but feel free to swap in your preferred bread. For a sweet flavor pairing, I recommend a smear of Rustic Peach Jam with Thyme topped with blackberries, a drizzle of agave, and a pinch of flaky sea salt. If you like a savory breakfast or brunch, try topping your toast with hummus, Smoky Roasted Carrots, capers, and everything bagel seasoning. With so many options, you can't go wrong.

1 Scoop the Rustic Peach Jam with Thyme, Smoky Roasted Carrots, hummus, and almond butter into four medium bowls and place them in the middle of your serving board.

2 Pour the flaky sea salt, everything bagel seasoning, capers, and agave nectar into four small bowls and place them near the right-center of the board.

3 Arrange the toast in an overlapping pattern along the top edge of the board.

4 Arrange the orange slices in an overlapping pattern along the bottom edge of the board.

5 Use scissors to snip the grapes into individual clusters and pile half of them together along the edge of the board next to the orange slices. Pile the other half next to the toast.

6 Fan the radishes along the edge of the board next to the toast and grapes. Place the avocado between the grapes, radishes, and orange slices.

7 Complete the perimeter by adding a handful of microgreens next to the grapes. Place the two kiwi halves near the toast.

8 Use a back-and-forth folding action with the cucumber ribbons and line them up to create a cucumber river between the toast and hummus.

9 Use the blackberries to fill in gaps left on the board between the bowls and other ingredients. Garnish the board with fresh dill.

Breakfast in Bed Board

SERVES 1 OR 2

Fills a 14-inch (35 cm) round board

1 cup (140 g) straw-
    berries, halved
1 cup (240 ml) fresh
    squeezed juice
1 tablespoon (14 g)
    vegan butter
1 tablespoon (14 g)
    raspberry jam
1 batch Chickpea
    Scramble with
    Mushrooms
    (page 138)
1 slice bread, toasted
½ avocado, sliced

Unless you have a hard-and-fast rule about not eating in bed, you've probably dreamt about waking up to a warm, homemade breakfast next to your pillow. Let your loved one linger in bed a bit longer with this Breakfast in Bed Board. Whether it's a birthday, an anniversary, or a holiday, breakfast in bed is such a special way to show how much you care. This Breakfast in Bed Board feeds one hungry late riser or two as a morning grazing board. I recommend serving with two forks in case the recipient of your affection feels generous and invites you to share.

1 Transfer the sliced strawberries to a small bowl and place it in the upper right corner of the serving board. Pour the juice into a glass and place it near the top of the board next to a bud vase with fresh flowers.

2 Scoop the vegan butter and raspberry jam into mini bowls and place them near the juice.

3 When the Chickpea Scramble with Mushrooms is nearly done cooking, pop a slice of bread in your toaster. When done, slice the toast in half diagonally.

4 Transfer the chickpea scramble to a plate and place it in the bottom left corner of the serving board. Set the toast next to the scramble and layer the avocado slices in the upper left corner of the board.

Grab-and-Go Oatmeal Board

SERVES 4

Fills a 16 x 24-inch (40 x 60 cm) board or marble pastry slab

1 batch Instant Pot
  Vegan Oatmeal
  (page 140) or other
  oatmeal of your
  choosing
½ cup (120 g) creamy
  peanut butter
½ cup (90 g) vegan
  chocolate chips
½ cup (75 g) candied
  pecans
½ cup (50 g) coconut
  chips
½ cup (60 g) dried
  cranberries
½ cup (75 g) pistachios
⅓ cup (45 g) raw
  pumpkin seeds
2 tablespoons (30 ml)
  maple syrup
2 tablespoons (16 g)
  ground cinnamon
Juice of ½ lemon
1 apple
1 banana

Whether you're trying to feed your family before everyone scoots out the door or you have a house full of overnight guests, mornings can be hectic. Enter the humble bowl of oatmeal. This Grab-and-Go Oatmeal Board features toppings and mix-ins that will please everyone passing through your kitchen. Thanks to the Instant Pot, the oatmeal recipe on this board is completely hands-off, giving you a solid 30 minutes to slice fruit and fill bowls with nuts, seeds, and syrup; if you do not have an Instant Pot, simply substitute another homemade oatmeal that you like. Serve with a stack of individual compostable bowls and spoons for a truly portable breakfast that is a snap to clean up.

1 If you have an Instant Pot or a similar electric pressure cooker, let it do the work cooking the oatmeal while you prepare the rest of the board components. If you do not have such an appliance, make 4 cups (600 g) cooked oatmeal with whatever recipe you prefer.

2 Transfer the peanut butter, chocolate chips, candied pecans, coconut chips, cranberries, and pistachios into small bowls.

3 Add the pumpkin seeds to a slightly smaller bowl and pour the maple syrup and cinnamon into mini bowls.

4 Scoop the warm, cooked oatmeal into a medium bowl and place it in the center of your serving board. Set the bowls of toppings around the oatmeal.

5 Pour the lemon juice into a medium-size bowl. Dice the apple and toss with the lemon juice right away to prevent browning. Repeat this process with the banana and place the sliced fruit on the board just before serving.

6 Set compostable bowls and spoons in the lower left corner of the board or off to the side of the board so your family and guests can build their own breakfasts on their way out the door.

Sweet and Spicy Melon Sparkler Board

SERVES 4

Fills an 11 x 16-inch (28 x 40 cm) rectangular board

2 cups (480 ml)
   watermelon juice

2 cups (480 ml)
   cantaloupe juice

½ cup (120 ml) orange
   juice or agave nectar

2 jalapeños, sliced

2 mini seedless
   cucumbers, sliced

1 bunch fresh mint

2 limes, quartered

1 (750 ml) bottle
   sparkling wine

1 (750 ml) bottle
   sparkling water
   (optional)

1 bucket of ice

You don't need a juicer to make these luscious, sparkling melon cocktails. Simply add watermelon or cantaloupe to your blender and blitz to liquefy the fruit, then pour the juice through a fine-mesh strainer into a carafe. While you can find watermelon and cantaloupe in stores year-round, the best time to buy these juicy fruits is in the summer. The sweetest melons, which are arguably the best melons, will feel heavy for their size. Make this Sweet and Spicy Melon Sparkler Board for a small wedding shower, brunch, or birthday celebration.

1 Place four cocktail glasses on your serving board.

2 Set a 16-ounce (480 ml) carafe of watermelon juice and a 16-ounce (480 ml) carafe of cantaloupe juice in the upper right corner of the board. (See full photo on page 18.)

3 Pour the orange juice or agave nectar into a small creamer or pitcher and place it near the lower left corner of the board.

4 Add clusters of jalapeño and cucumber slices at the top, middle, and bottom of the board. Tuck fresh mint leaves in around the glasses and place lime wedges near the cucumber.

5 Pop a bottle of sparkling wine and set it off to the side of the board. Serve with sparkling water for a nonalcoholic option, if desired. Place the bucket of ice next to the board.

For 1 sweet sparkler:

1 mint leaf
1½ ounces (42 g) melon juice
½ ounce (14 g) agave nectar or
    orange juice
3 ounces (84 g) sparkling wine
Squeeze of lime juice
Cucumber slice, for garnish

1 Place the mint leaf in the
    bottom of a glass and muddle
    with a spoon.

2 Pour in your choice of melon
    juice, agave nectar or orange
    juice, and sparkling wine. Stir to
    mix the ingredients, then add ice.

3 Finish off your sparkler with a
    squeeze of lime juice and a slice
    of cucumber.

For 1 spicy sparkler:

1 mint leaf
1 jalapeño slice, seeds removed
1½ ounces (42 g) melon juice
½ ounce (14 g) agave nectar or
    orange juice
3 ounces (84 g) sparkling wine
Squeeze of lime juice
Cucumber slice, for garnish

1 Place the mint leaf and jalapeño
    in the bottom of a glass and
    muddle with a spoon.

2 Pour in your choice of melon
    juice, agave nectar or orange
    juice, and sparkling wine. Stir to
    mix the ingredients, then add ice.

3 Finish off your sparkler with a
    squeeze of lime juice and a slice
    of cucumber.

Vegan Breakfast Burrito Board

SERVES 4
Fills a 20-inch (50 cm) round board

1 batch Chickpea
    Scramble with
    Mushrooms
    (page 138)
4 burrito-size tortillas,
    (or collard green
    leaves for a
    gluten-free option)
4 cups (120 g) baby
    spinach
1 cup (240 g) pico de
    gallo or salsa
½ red onion, chopped
1 (15-ounce [420 g])
    can black beans,
    drained and rinsed
Pinch of salt
1 bunch cilantro,
    chopped
2 tomatoes, diced
2 tablespoons (30 ml)
    hot sauce
1 red bell pepper,
    cored and sliced
1 avocado, peeled,
    pitted, and sliced
1 lime, quartered

When I lived in Chicago, my roommates and I would often gather in the kitchen on Saturday mornings and make breakfast burritos. Each person was in charge of chopping, sautéing, or toasting one of the burrito components. At the end, we lined everything up on the countertop and built our own breakfast burritos. The collaborative aspect of making a meal together, combined with lots of coffee and good music, always inspired the best chats.

1 Preheat your oven to 200°F (100°C or gas mark ½). Make the Chickpea Scramble with Mushrooms and place it in the oven to keep warm until you're ready to serve. Set a medium bowl or plate in the center of the board as a placeholder for the scramble.

2 Warm a large, dry skillet over medium-low heat and toast the tortillas one at a time. Transfer the tortillas to a plate and cover with a kitchen towel to keep them warm until ready to serve. If you're using collard green leaves, place them directly on the board.

3 Divide the baby spinach into two clusters and place them on the board.

4 Pour the pico de gallo into a small bowl and set it on the board. Scoop the chopped red onion into another small bowl and place it near the pico de gallo.

5 Warm the black beans on the stovetop, add a pinch of salt, and transfer to a medium serving bowl. Set it on the board near the onion and pico de gallo.

6 Put the chopped cilantro in a small bowl and place it on the board by the black beans. Scoop the diced tomato into a small bowl and set it on the board.

7 Pour the hot sauce into a mini bowl and place it on the board.

8 Divide the red bell pepper slices into clusters and place them across the board along with the avocado slices.

9 Fold the tortillas in half and layer them on the right side of the board.

10 Transfer the Chickpea Scramble with Mushrooms to the bowl or plate in the middle of the board. Fill in any small gaps with lime wedges.

Sweet Potato Breakfast Bowls Board

SERVES 4

Fills an 11 x 16-inch (28 x 40 cm) rectangular board

1 batch Whipped Sweet
   Potato and Carrots
   (page 151)

2 (5-ounce [140 g])
   containers dairy-free
   vanilla yogurt

1 cup (240 g) almond
   butter

½ cup (60 g) granola

½ pint (150 g)
   blueberries

6 ounces (168 g)
   raspberries

¼ cup (60 ml) maple
   syrup

1 yellow bell pepper,
   cored and diced

4 scallions, thinly sliced

2 tablespoons (30 ml)
   hot sauce

1 ounce (28 g)
   everything bagel
   seasoning

1 ounce (28 g) flaky
   sea salt

1 avocado, peeled,
   pitted, and diced

1 banana

Juice of ½ lemon

Delight your breakfast or brunch guests with this high-vibe morning meal. A bed of velvety whipped root veggies provides a colorful and surprising base for sweet and savory toppings. The Whipped Sweet Potato and Carrots can be prepared the day before so you can focus on building a gorgeous board the morning of. Rather than separate the sweet and savory mix-ins on opposite sides of the board, place them next to one another to encourage your family and friends to experiment with interesting flavor combinations. Bonus: This colorful board is a great way to use up leftover fruits and vegetables at the end of the week.

1 Make the Whipped Sweet Potato and Carrots and scoop into a medium serving bowl. Set it in the center of your board.

2 Pour the dairy-free yogurt, almond butter, and granola into small bowls and stagger them on the board. Spill the blueberries and raspberries directly on the board.

3 Pour the maple syrup into a mini bowl and set it on the board.

4 Transfer the diced bell pepper to a small bowl and set it on the board.

5 Fill mini bowls with hot sauce, everything bagel seasoning, and flaky sea salt and set the bowls near the sweet toppings on the board.

6 Transfer the diced avocado to a small bowl and set it on the board.

7 Peel the banana and slice it into ½-inch (13 mm) pieces. Drizzle the banana with lemon juice to prevent it from browning and set it on the board.

Build-Your-Own Bagel Sandwich Board

SERVES 6

Fills a 14 x 27-inch (35 x 70 cm) rectangular board

6 bagels, sliced in half

1 batch Roasted Beet Hummus (page 132)

1 (8-ounce [227 g]) container plain vegan cream cheese

1 (8-ounce [227 g]) container scallion vegan cream cheese

1 tablespoon (6 g) finely chopped fresh scallion

1 (7-ounce [196 g]) bag fresh arugula

1 large cucumber, sliced

2 large tomatoes, sliced

½ red onion, sliced into rounds

1 avocado, peeled, pitted, and sliced

½ ounce (42 g) alfalfa sprouts

2 tablespoons (30 ml) hot sauce

¼ cup (56 g) vegan butter

¼ cup (30 g) everything bagel seasoning

1 small orange

When it comes to circular breakfast foods, I have always preferred a warm, chewy bagel slathered with savory cream cheese over a donut. While I'm not sure my friends and family share this preference, they're always excited when I set this Build-Your-Own Bagel Sandwich Board on the kitchen table. Bagels are a sturdy, satisfying vessel for vegan cream cheese, hummus, and veggies. Pick up a half dozen from your local bakery or bagel shop the morning of your gathering for the freshest taste and texture. Your brunch guests will enjoy selecting their spreads and toppings between sips of coffee, juice, or mimosas.

1 Toast the bagels and arrange them down the center of your board.

2 Scoop the Roasted Beet Hummus, plain vegan cream cheese, and scallion vegan cream cheese into bowls of similar size and set them across the board. Sprinkle the chopped scallion on top of the scallion cream cheese.

3 Place clumps of arugula in five or six different places on the board.

4 Fan the cucumber slices near the scallion vegan cream cheese.

5 Layer the tomato slices on small plates and set them on the board.

6 Pile the sliced red onion on top of the arugula.

7 Divide the avocado slices into clusters and set them on the board.

8 Add a large pile of alfalfa sprouts to the board, overlapping the arugula.

9 Pour the hot sauce into a mini bowl and set it on the board.

10 Transfer the vegan butter and everything bagel seasoning to mini bowls and set them on the board.

11 Slice the orange in half and place it on the board.

CHAPTER 2

Grazing at Home Boards

Mediterranean
Grazing Board
39

Ombré Farmers'
Market Board
40

Pantry Essentials
Snack Board
43

Stone Fruit Panzanella
Salad Board
45

Vegan Banh Mi
Board
46

Afternoon Tapas
and Sangria Board
48

Loaded Sweet Potato
Fries Board
51

Netflix Night
for Two Board
52

Front Yard Picnic
Board
55

Family Movie
Night Board
56

Date Night Vegan
Cheese Board
58

Backyard
Campfire Board
60

Post-Workout
Lunch Board
63

Overnight Guest
Welcome Board
64

Friday Happy Hour
Board
67

◄◄ Sweet Potato Brownie Bowl, Netflix Night
for Two Board (page 52)

Mediterranean Grazing Board

SERVES 6 TO 8

Fills a 20-inch (50 cm) round board

1 batch Quinoa Tabbouleh
　Salad (page 131)
1 cucumber, thinly sliced
3 pita breads, sliced into
　triangles
1 batch Roasted Red
　Pepper Hummus
　(page 132)
16 wheat crackers
1 cup (140 g) pomegranate
　arils
½ cup (70 g) manzanilla
　olives, drained
½ cup (70 g) kalamata
　olives, drained
1 (8-ounce [240 g]) jar
　marinated artichokes,
　drained
1 (9.5-ounce [266 g]) jar
　olive tapenade
1 cup (240 g) Quick Pickled
　Red Onions (page 145)
¼ cup (35 g) capers
1 bunch radishes, trimmed
　and halved
10 figs, halved
2 cups (260 g) dried
　apricots
1 lemon, sliced into wedges
6 ounces (168 g) cherry
　tomatoes on the vine
Fresh mint leaves

The countries surrounding the Mediterranean Sea are known for their abundance of fresh vegetables, wheat, olive oil, and herbs. Of course, this is a broad description of what the region has to offer; Mediterranean food is extremely diverse and it would be impossible to capture the influence of every culture on one board. Here, you'll find familiar favorites like pita bread, hummus, and olives. My take on tabbouleh, a Middle Eastern salad, uses quinoa instead of the traditional bulgur, making it suitable for those with gluten allergies and sensitivities.

1　Scoop the Quinoa Tabbouleh Salad into a medium bowl and place it near the left-center of the board. Fan the cucumber and most of the pita bread around the tabbouleh.

2　Transfer the Roasted Red Pepper Hummus to a small bowl and set it on the opposite side of the board. Fan the wheat crackers around the bowl.

3　Spoon the pomegranate arils, olives, artichokes, olive tapenade, and pickled onions into small bowls and set them on the board. Fan the remaining pita bread along the edge of the board between the olive tapenade and the hummus.

4　Fill in gaps on the board with the radishes, figs, dried apricots, and lemon wedges. Place the cherry tomatoes in a small bowl off to the side and garnish the board with fresh mint.

Ombré Farmers' Market Board

SERVES 4

Fills an 11 x 16-inch (28 x 40 cm) rectangular board

1 batch Roasted Beet Hummus (page 132)

1 batch Strawberry Cashew Cheesecake Dip (page 133)

1 cup (140 g) pomegranate arils

1½ cups (225 g) cherries

6 figs

2 cups (300 g) strawberries

12 ounces (336 g) Easter egg radishes

8 ounces (227 g) cherry tomatoes on the vine

8 to 10 red mini sweet peppers

1 yellow peach, pitted and sliced

8 small slices watermelon

This board is stuffed with a gradient of rosy produce straight from the local farmers' market. From super-sweet cherries to perfectly ripe cherry tomatoes, this antioxidant-rich fruit and veggie board features a variety of sizes, shapes, and textures for your guests to explore. On the savory side of things, Roasted Beet Hummus steals the show with a vibrant pinkish-red hue and an earthy, yet complex, flavor. The Strawberry Cashew Cheesecake Dip is sweet and decadent, yet light, and could even pass as a healthy dessert.

1 Scoop the Roasted Beet Hummus and Strawberry Cashew Cheesecake Dip into small bowls. Place the hummus toward the middle of the board and the dip toward the bottom of the board.

2 Pour the pomegranate arils into a smaller bowl and place at the top of the board.

3 The fruits and veggies gradually fade from dark to light as the eye wanders down the board. Place the darkest fruits—the cherries and figs—at the top of the board around the pomegranate arils.

4 Add the strawberries, radishes, tomatoes, and sweet peppers to the middle of the board next to the hummus.

5 Place the sliced peach and watermelon at the bottom of the board near the Strawberry Cashew Cheesecake Dip.

Pantry Essentials Snack Board

SERVES 6

Fills an 11 x 16-inch (28 x 40 cm) rectangular board

1 batch Crispy Spiced
   Chickpeas (page 138)
3 cups (450 g) dried fruit
   (dried cranberries,
   dried apricots, raisins,
   dates)
2 cups (300 g) nuts and/or
   seeds (walnuts,
   pistachios, almonds,
   macadamia nuts,
   sunflower seeds,
   pumpkin seeds)
1 cup (140 g) olives or
   sliced pickles
½ cup (120 g) jam or
   fruit spread
½ cup (120 g) nut butter
   or sunflower seed
   butter
1 (12-ounce [340 g])
   box crackers

Before you head to the grocery store for a snack haul, check your cupboard to see what leftover nuts, dried fruit, and crackers can be put to use on this Pantry Essentials Snack Board. I'm willing to bet you can create an appealing, plant-based board with items you already have at home. A humble can of chickpeas becomes an irresistibly crispy snack when roasted and tossed with spices. Dig around for an unopened jar of olives or pickles, or reach into your fridge and clear out your condiment shelf. This board is all about using what you already have at home to create a flavorful spread of sweet and savory snacks.

1 Place four or five small bowls on your serving board. Fill each one with Crispy Spiced Chickpeas, dried cranberries or raisins, nuts, and seeds. Place larger dried fruits, like dried apricots and dates, directly on the board.

2 Place the olives or pickles in a slightly smaller bowl and set it in the lower left corner of the board.

3 Scoop the jam and nut butter into small bowls and place them near the top of the board.

4 Create a "river" of crackers that flows across the width of the board near the jam and nut butter.

5 Serve the board with a few small bowls that everyone can fill with their favorite snacks and enjoy throughout the day.

Stone Fruit Panzanella Salad Board

SERVES 6
Fills a 20-inch (50 cm) round board

If you require a side of freshly baked bread to enjoy a salad, you're going to adore panzanella, a Tuscan salad made with chunks of stale bread, tomatoes, and onion. The bread cubes soften as they soak up juice from the tomatoes and take on a delightful flavor and texture. This Stone Fruit Panzanella Salad Board is inspired by traditional panzanella with a few seasonal surprises. Peaches and cherries play right into the fresh summer flavors already present in classic panzanella, while a sprinkle of crunchy, flaky sea salt makes the entire dish sing. If you can, allow the bread cubes to soak in the tomato juices and dressing for at least a half hour before serving.

6 cups (420 g) cubed hearty, day-old bread

2 ripe tomatoes on the vine, cored and diced

1 batch Red Wine Vinaigrette (page 146), divided

2 yellow peaches, pitted and sliced

1½ cups (225 g) sweet cherries, halved and pitted

2 medium cucumbers

1 pound (454 g) heirloom cherry tomatoes, halved

2 tablespoons (30 g) flaky sea salt

2 tablespoons (16 g) capers, drained

½ red onion, thinly sliced

1 large bunch fresh basil leaves

1 Place the bread cubes in a large serving bowl. Add the diced tomatoes and ¼ cup (60 ml) of the Red Wine Vinaigrette. Toss to coat the bread in the tomato juices and dressing and place the bowl on the lower right side of the board.

2 Add the sliced peaches to a medium bowl and place it at the top of the board. Place the cherries in a small bowl toward the bottom of the board near the bread.

3 Slice the cucumbers in half lengthwise and trim the ends. Use a spoon to scoop out the fleshy center of the cucumber halves and discard. Slice the cucumbers into ¼-inch (6 mm) half-moons and place them in a medium bowl just above the cherries.

4 Place the cherry tomatoes in a medium bowl in the upper right corner of the board above the bread.

5 Pour the flaky sea salt and capers into mini bowls and place them at the top of the board.

6 Layer the onion slices on a small appetizer plate and place it at the top of the board by the capers and salt. Transfer the remaining Red Wine Vinaigrette to a cruet or an oil dispenser and place it at the top of the board.

7 Add clusters of fresh basil all around the board and add a few small basil leaves to the bowl with the bread cubes.

8 Let guests build their salad however they see fit.

Vegan Banh Mi Board

SERVES 4

Fills an 11 x 16-inch (28 x 40 cm) rectangular board

1 fresh French baguette

¼ cup (60 g) vegan mayo

1 batch Banh Mi Pulled Jackfruit (page 135)

2 jalapeños, sliced into rounds

1 batch Quick Pickled Carrots (page 145)

½ cucumber, sliced

½ bunch cilantro

In Vietnamese cuisine, banh mi is a sandwich made on a baguette that is perfectly crisp on the outside and soft and fluffy on the inside. The bread is the focal point of the sandwich, so I recommend picking up a loaf baked fresh the morning you plan to serve this Vegan Banh Mi Board. While I can't claim any sort of authenticity, many of the fixings for a traditional banh mi are included on this board to allow your family and friends to sample Vietnamese-inspired food without hopping on a plane. Spread each sandwich with vegan mayo and stuff with Banh Mi Pulled Jackfruit, Quick Pickled Carrots, cilantro, jalapeño, and cucumber. The flavor combination is salty, savory, and refreshing.

1 Slice the baguette into four equal pieces. Then cut each piece almost all the way in half lengthwise, leaving about ½ inch (1.3 cm) of the bread intact. Place the sandwich loaves on the board.

2 Spoon the vegan mayo into a mini bowl and place it at the top of the board.

3 Transfer the Banh Mi Pulled Jackfruit to a bowl and place it in the middle of the board.

4 Layer the jalapeño slices on an appetizer plate and set it on the board.

5 Use tongs to transfer the Quick Pickled Carrots to a small bowl, leaving excess pickling liquid behind in the jar, and place the bowl on the board.

6 Arrange the cucumber slices in clusters at the top, middle, and bottom of the board. Fill in large gaps on the board with clusters of cilantro.

7 To assemble a sandwich, open the baguette and spread 1 tablespoon (15 g) of vegan mayo on the bottom half. Add a layer of cucumber followed by pickled carrot, jalapeño, Banh Mi Pulled Jackfruit, and cilantro.

Afternoon Tapas and Sangria Board

SERVES 4

Fills a 20-inch (50 cm) round board

1 batch Pan con
Tomate (page 143)

1 batch Pimentón
Roasted Carrots
(page 144)

1 (9.5-ounce [266 g])
jar olive tapenade

20 stone ground wheat
crackers

6 ounces (168 g)
roasted and salted
Marcona almonds

1 (10-ounce [280 g])
package grilled
artichoke halves

4 ounces (112 g)
manzanilla olives

8 ounces (227 g) red
seedless grapes

1 batch Red Sangria
(page 145)

1 (750 ml) bottle cava
(optional)

This board was inspired by a trip to Barcelona in my early twenties. My family, fresh off a ten-hour flight from Chicago, wasted no time stumbling into a restaurant for our first taste of tapas (Spanish snacks) and sangria. I'm not sure whether it was the jet lag, the wine, or a combination of the two, but we chatted and laughed for hours on the patio. The tapas on this board are designed to be eaten at room temperature, perfect for leisurely grazing while sipping sangria. I like to top off my glass of sangria with a splash of cava, which is Spanish sparkling wine. Consider opening a bottle and serving it with your tapas and sangria for others to do the same.

1 Layer the toasted ciabatta for the Pan con Tomate in two rows on the right side of your serving board. Place the grated tomato, olive oil, and flaky sea salt beside it.

2 Transfer the Pimentón Roasted Carrots to a salad or dinner plate and set it on the upper left side of the board.

3 Scoop the olive tapenade into a small bowl and set it on the board. Fan the crackers around it.

4 Put the almonds, artichoke halves, and olives in small bowls and place them in the lower left corner of the board near the tapenade.

5 Snip the grapes into small clusters for easy grabbing and use them to fill in any large gaps on the board.

6 Serve with a pitcher of Red Sangria and a bottle of cava, if desired.

Loaded Sweet Potato Fries Board

SERVES 6
Fills a 20-inch (50 cm) round board

1 batch Vegan Cheese Sauce (page 134)

2 cups (500 g) Cincinnati-Style Vegan Chili (page 130) or 1 (14.7-ounce [412 g]) can vegan chili, warmed

½ cup (120 g) ketchup

1 bunch scallions, thinly sliced

1 cup (150 g) corn, warmed

1 (15-ounce [420 g]) can black beans, drained, rinsed, and warmed

1½ cups (210 g) chopped tomato

1 cup (240 g) salsa

1 (20-ounce [560 g]) bag sweet potato waffle fries

1 (15-ounce [420 g]) bag frozen sweet potato fries

Make your favorite restaurant appetizer at home with the Loaded Sweet Potato Fries Board. Sweet potato waffle fries in particular, with their wide and flat shape, are the best type of fries for eating with toppings. Keep it simple with ketchup or load up your pile of fries with savory sauces and veggies. The combination of Vegan Cheese Sauce and Cincinnati-Style Vegan Chili is sure to be popular, so consider making more than you think is necessary. Any leftovers can be stored in the fridge and enjoyed on another board. As a general rule, sweet potato fries have the best flavor and texture right after they come out of the oven, so make them just before serving.

1 Set two bowls in the center of the board as placeholders for the Vegan Cheese Sauce and Cincinnati-Style Vegan Chili.

2 Make the Vegan Cheese Sauce and Cincinnati-Style Vegan Chili and cover to keep warm. If you're using canned vegan chili, simmer it on the stove according to the can directions.

3 Squirt the ketchup into a small bowl.

4 Transfer the sliced scallions, corn, black beans, tomato, and salsa to slightly larger bowls. Place them on the board next to the chili and cheese sauce bowls.

5 Bake the sweet potato waffle fries and sweet potato fries according to the package directions. Allow them to cool for a few minutes on the baking sheet before transferring them to the board.

6 Pour the warm Vegan Cheese Sauce and Cincinnati-Style Vegan Chili into their respective bowls and serve immediately.

Netflix Night for Two Board

SERVES 2

Fills an 11 x 16-inch (28 x 40 cm) rectangular board

1 batch Sweet Potato
    Brownie Bowls
    (page 148)
1 batch Lemon
    Artichoke Dip
    (page 140)
1 (17.6-ounce [495 g])
    jar giant Halkidiki
    olives, drained
½ cup (75 g) raw
    pistachios
1 (5-ounce [140 g])
    package roasted
    and salted Marcona
    almonds
½ cup (120 ml)
    marinara sauce,
    warmed
1 (3.4-ounce [95
    g]) package rice
    crackers
8 ounces (240 g)
    champagne grapes
6 Italian breadsticks
    with olive oil

If your idea of a relaxing Friday night (or any night, for that matter) is settling in to the couch for a movie marathon with your loved one, there's a board for that. This Netflix Night for Two Board has all of your sweet, salty, and savory cravings covered, so there's no need to hit pause and run to the kitchen. Individual Sweet Potato Brownie Bowls eliminate the awkward fight over the last bite of dessert, while olives, crackers, and nuts satisfy the desire to munch through those intense plot twists. Serve with your favorite beverage for a cozy night at home.

1 Bake the Sweet Potato Brownie Bowls while you prep the rest of the board components.

2 Scoop the Lemon Artichoke Dip into a small bowl and place it on the board.

3 Place the olives, pistachios, almonds, and marinara sauce in slightly smaller bowls and place them across the board. Use the bowls as bookends to hold clusters of the rice crackers in place.

4 When the Sweet Potato Brownie Bowls are done baking, set two small trivets or coasters on the board to protect the surface and place the brownie bowls on top of them.

5 Fill in gaps on the board with the champagne grapes and tuck a few breadsticks in on opposite sides of the board.

Front Yard Picnic Board

SERVES 4
Fills a 14 x 27-inch (35 x 70 cm) rectangular board

1 pound (454 g) vegan pasta salad, homemade or store-bought

4 Chickpea Salad Sandwiches (page 137)

2 peaches, pitted and sliced into wedges

1 cup (240 ml) vegan ranch dressing

8 ounces (240 g) carrots, peeled and cut into sticks

1 head of celery, cut into sticks

1 (16-ounce [454 g]) bag pretzels

1 quart (1 L) homemade lemonade

You don't need to pack up the car and drive to the beach or wait for a table at your local restaurant to dine outdoors. Set down a comfy blanket in your front yard (or anywhere you can find a patch of grass) and enjoy a meal al fresco with this Front Yard Picnic Board. Though it may seem over the top for a laid-back lunch, I like using the largest board I have to allow everyone a place at the "table." Make a few sandwiches, slice up some fruits and veggies, and pick up a pound of pasta salad for a classic picnic feast. Tip: If you're going the store-bought route, Whole Foods clearly labels vegan items on its salad bar.

1. Scoop the vegan pasta salad into a medium serving bowl and set it on the board.

2. Slice the Chickpea Salad Sandwiches in half and line them up down the center of the board.

3. Cluster the peach slices on the board.

4. Pour the vegan ranch dressing into a small bowl and place it on the board. Group the carrot and celery sticks in four clusters each across the board.

5. Fill in any gaps on the board with pretzels, overlapping the fruits and veggies if necessary.

6. Serve with homemade lemonade.

Family Movie Night Board

SERVES 4 TO 6
Fills a 20-inch (50 cm) round board

1 batch Savory Dill
   Popcorn (page 147)
1 cup (240 g) vegan
   chocolate hazelnut
   spread
1 (10-ounce [280 g])
   container hummus
12 ounces (340 g)
   baby carrots
1 (3.4-ounce [95
   g]) package rice
   crackers
Juice of ½ lemon
2 apples
1 batch Crispy
   Spiced Chickpeas
   (page 138)
8 ounces (227 g)
   red grapes
8 ounces (227 g)
   green grapes

Let the kids choose a movie while you prep this Family Movie Night Board. Popcorn, the quintessential movie snack, gets a savory upgrade with dill and nutritional yeast, while sliced apple and vegan chocolate hazelnut spread will satisfy everyone's sweet tooth. Don't skip the Crispy Spiced Chickpeas—they're crisp on the outside and chewy on the inside and a perfect texture contrast to the crunchy snacks across the board. Baby carrots and grapes add a fresh element to this movie night spread and offer an extra serving of fruits and veggies for the day.

1 Transfer the Savory Dill Popcorn to a large serving bowl and place it on the board.

2 Scoop the vegan chocolate hazelnut spread into a small bowl and place it on the board.

3 Scoop the hummus into another small bowl and set it on the opposite side of the board from the vegan chocolate hazelnut spread.

4 Place clusters of baby carrots and rice crackers across the board, concentrating on the area surrounding the hummus.

5 Pour the lemon juice into a bowl. Core and slice the apples and immediately toss the pieces with the lemon juice to prevent browning. Arrange the apple slices in clusters across the board.

6 Transfer the Crispy Spiced Chickpeas to a small bowl and set it on the board.

7 Add clusters of red and green grapes to the board, filling in any gaps.

Date Night Vegan Cheese Board

SERVES 2

Fill an 11 x 16-inch (28 x 40 cm) rectangular board

1 semi-firm vegan
cheese wheel,
such as a Miyoko's
Creamery

1 (5-ounce [140 g])
container vegan
cheese spread,
such as a Kite Hill
or Plant Perks

1 soft vegan cheese,
such as Treeline
French-Style

1 (11-ounce [308 g])
jar fig butter

1 (17.6-ounce [495 g])
jar giant Halkidiki
olives, drained

1 sliced vegan cheese,
such as Chao
Creamery

1 (4.4-ounce [125 g])
box water crackers

1 demi ciabatta
baguette, sliced

1 cup (100 g) candied
pecans

2 mandarin oranges,
cut in half crosswise

Fresh rosemary sprigs,
for garnish

If you're not typically one to splurge on fancy vegan cheeses, consider treating yourself. This Date Night Vegan Cheese Board is all about indulging and trying those plant-based products you've been eyeing at the grocery store. Your choices will depend on what's available in your part of the world, but I've included some guidelines to help you curate a well-rounded selection. Vegan cheese can be quite rich and flavorful, so you'll want to include some palate cleansers on the board to get the full tasting experience. Sliced baguette, olives, and mandarin oranges make terrific choices. Wrap up leftover vegan cheese and save it in the refrigerator for another date night.

1 Set a square of wax paper or parchment paper on the board. Unwrap the vegan cheese wheel and place it on top of it.

2 Scoop the vegan cheese spread into a bowl and place it on the board.

3 Scoop the soft vegan cheese into a bowl and place it on the opposite side of the board from the vegan cheese spread.

4 Scoop the fig butter into a small bowl and place it near the soft vegan cheese.

5 Place the olives in a medium bowl and set it at the top of the board.

6 Cut the vegan cheese slices into squares and fan them on the board.

7 Add clusters of water crackers across the board next to each vegan cheese.

8 Fan the baguette slices in groups at the top and bottom of the board. Add clusters of pecans near the baguette.

9 Place the mandarin orange halves on the board and garnish with fresh rosemary sprigs.

Backyard Campfire Board

SERVES 12
Fills a 20-inch (50 cm) round board

6 Carrot Dogs (page 128) or vegan hot dogs

2 cups (300 g) trail mix

½ cup (120 g) creamy salted peanut butter

½ cup (120 g) vegan chocolate hazelnut spread

⅓ cup (80 ml) ketchup

¼ cup (60 ml) mustard

1 (14-ounce [392 g]) box vegan graham crackers

3 (3-ounce [85 g]) vegan chocolate bars

1 pound (455 g) strawberries

1 (10-ounce [280 g]) bag vegan marshmallows

6 whole wheat hot dog buns

Many of my cherished memories with family and friends involve sitting around a campfire. Whether we're playing guitar, telling stories, stargazing, or simply enjoying the quiet flicker of the flames, there's something special about gathering around a firepit and sharing an evening outdoors. This Backyard Campfire Board is designed to enhance the communal aspect of chilly fall nights. I recommend precooking the vegan hot dogs or Carrot Dogs and warming them on a stick over the fire just before serving. Of course, all of the fixings for vegan s'mores are here, too.

1 If you're making the Carrot Dogs, boil and marinate them at least four hours before cooking and serving. If you're serving vegan hot dogs from a package, skip this step.

2 Pour the trail mix into a medium bowl and set it on the board.

3 Scoop the peanut butter and vegan chocolate hazelnut spread into bowls of similar size and place them on the board.

4 Squirt the ketchup and mustard into mini bowls and place them on the board.

5 Break the vegan graham crackers into squares and layer them in clusters across the board. Break the vegan chocolate bars into squares and place them on the board.

6 Divide the strawberries into clusters and layer them on top of the graham crackers and chocolate.

7 Spill the bag of vegan marshmallows directly onto the board, overlapping the graham crackers and chocolate.

8 Cook the Carrot Dogs. If you're making vegan hot dogs, cook them according to the package directions. When cool enough to handle, slice the Carrot Dogs or vegan hot dogs in half crosswise.

9 Trim the ends of each hot dog bun to fit the size of your Carrot Dogs or vegan hot dogs. Then slice the buns in half crosswise. Wedge a piece of Carrot Dog or vegan hot dog into each bun segment and place them on the board.

Post-Workout Lunch Board

SERVES 2
Fills an 11 x 16-inch (28 x 40 cm) rectangular board

⅔ cup (160 g) hummus

1 tablespoon (8 g) hulled hemp seeds

4 celery stalks, sliced

1 cup (150 g) berries

½ cup (70 g) shelled edamame, cooked

1 Lemon Blueberry Quinoa Muffin (page 141)

¼ cup (35 g) raw almonds

1 (16-ounce [480 ml]) carafe filtered, fruit-infused water

Dietitians agree that a post-workout snack or meal should contain carbohydrates and protein. This Post-Workout Lunch Board offers both in addition to hydrating fresh fruit and healthy fats. While a baked good may not seem like a healthy choice, this Lemon Blueberry Quinoa Muffin is made with whole grains and is free of refined sugar. An appropriate serving size for this board is half a muffin—split it with your workout partner. Berries, edamame, almonds, and celery with hummus round out this colorful and nutritious lunch spread that will help you refuel after exercise.

1 Scoop the hummus into a small bowl and place it on the board. Sprinkle the hemp seeds on top of the hummus and arrange the celery stalks around the bowl.

2 Rinse the berries and set them directly on the board.

3 Place the cooked edamame in a small bowl and set it on the board.

4 Set the Lemon Blueberry Quinoa Muffin on the board.

5 Pour the almonds on the board.

6 Serve with a carafe of filtered, fruit-infused water and two glasses.

Overnight Guest Welcome Board

SERVES 2
Fills a 14-inch (35 cm) round board

2 Lemon Blueberry
  Quinoa Muffins
  (page 141)
½ lemon, sliced
1 (16-ounce [454 g])
  carafe filtered water
2 bananas
2 cups (300 g) trail mix
1 pint (300 g) fresh
  berries
2 (11-ounce [308 g])
  cans cold brew
  coffee

Whether you're hosting family, friends, or vacation rental guests, your goal is to provide a comfortable place to recharge and refuel after a long day of travel. In addition to the obvious amenities—fresh bedding and toiletries—this Overnight Guest Welcome Board is an extra-special touch that will make your guests feel right at home. Instead of bottled water, offer your guests two glasses and a carafe of infused water. Homemade muffins, bananas and berries, trail mix, and coffee for the morning will ensure your visitors have everything they need for a relaxing stay.

1 Make the Lemon Blueberry Quinoa Muffins and set two muffins aside to cool. Place the leftovers in a resealable bag and freeze for future houseguests.

2 Cut two 6-inch (15 cm) squares of parchment paper and place the muffins in the center of each. Fold up the sides of the parchment paper and tie with a piece of string or twine. Set the wrapped muffins on the board.

3 Place the lemon slices in the carafe and fill with cold, filtered water at least 3 hours before your guests arrive. Keep the infused water cold in the fridge until ready to serve.

4 Place the bananas on the board.

5 Pour the trail mix into two (8-ounce [227 g]) mason jars and set them on the board.

6 Fill a bowl or porcelain berry box colander with fresh strawberries or blueberries and place it on the board.

7 Set the cold brew coffee cans on the board with a friendly note for your guests to help themselves to ice in the freezer.

Friday Happy Hour Board

SERVES 4

Fills a 16 x 24-inch (40 x 60 cm) board or marble pastry slab

1 cup (123 g) roasted pistachios

1 (6.5-ounce [182 g]) semi-firm vegan cheese wheel, such as Miyoko's Creamery

1 (10-ounce [280 g]) container hummus

1 (10-ounce [280 g]) jar Halkidiki olives, drained

1 (3.5-ounce [100 g]) box Italian breadsticks

1 (3.4-ounce [95 g]) box rice crackers

8 ounces (227 g) petite carrots, sliced in half lengthwise

Juice of ½ lemon

1 apple

8 ounces (227 g) green grapes

1 (750 ml) bottle wine

Nothing compares to that Friday afternoon feeling. Celebrate the end of a long week with this Friday Happy Hour Board. This no-fuss board takes just minutes to assemble, so you can slip into relaxation mode and enjoy your evening. Although it's called happy hour, my friends and I have been known to keep the drinks, snacks, and conversation flowing well into the night. This board offers both light bites and heartier snacks that will satiate everyone until dinner. I recommend chilling an extra bottle of wine in case you have a few more guests than originally planned.

1   Pour the pistachios into a small bowl and set it on the board.

2   Unwrap the vegan cheese wheel and set it on the board with a small cheese knife. Scoop the hummus and olives into small bowls and set them on the board.

3   Place the Italian breadsticks directly on the board.

4   Arrange half of the rice crackers near the hummus. Set the remaining crackers at the top of the board.

5   Divide the petite carrots into two clusters and place them on either side of the board.

6   Pour the lemon juice into a small bowl. Core and slice the apple and toss with the lemon juice immediately to prevent browning. Fan the apple slices on the board.

7   Snip the grapes into small clusters for easy grabbing. Fill in any gaps on the board with the grapes.

8   Serve with your favorite bottle of wine.

CHAPTER 3

Meal Boards

Coconut Peanut Noodle
Bowls Board
71

Taco Bowl
Tuesday Board
72

Sunday Night
Pasta Board
74

Build-Your-Own
Sloppy Joes Board
77

Cincinnati-Style Chili
Dinner Board
78

Teriyaki Cabbage
Wraps Board
80

Grilled Cheese
and Roasted Tomato
Soup Board
83

Coconut Chickpea
Curry Board
84

Loaded Vegan
Chili Board
86

Rainbow Chopped
Salad Board
88

◄◄ Hearty Pinto and Black Bean Chili,
Loaded Vegan Chili Board (page 86)

Coconut Peanut Noodle Bowls Board

SERVES 6

Fills a 14 x 27-inch (35 x 70 cm) rectangular board

1 (14-ounce [392 g])
   package rice
   noodles, prepared
   according to
   package directions
1 batch Coconut
   Peanut Noodle
   Sauce (page 131)
2 medium carrots,
   julienned
1 cup (50 g) bean
   sprouts
2 cups (140 g) shredded
   purple cabbage
1 cup (145 g) roasted
   cashews
1 cup (16 g) chopped
   cilantro
4 scallions, thinly sliced
2 tablespoon (16 g)
   sesame seeds
1 cup (240 g) vegan
   kimchi
1 cup (75 g) sugar
   snap peas, sliced
   lengthwise
2 tablespoons (30 ml)
   soy sauce
1 lime, sliced into
   wedges

Combine Asian-inspired ingredients of varying colors, flavors, and textures to create a nutritious bowl brimming with veggies. As is true with many vegan dishes, the star of these Coconut Peanut Noodle Bowls is the sauce. It's relatively simple, yet extremely flavorful. Tip: Don't skimp on the vegan kimchi. Not only does it provide unique taste and texture to this noodle dish, but it's also fermented, which means you'll get a healthy dose of probiotics with every bite.

1 Use tongs to transfer the rice noodles to a large bowl and set it on the serving board. Scoop the Coconut Peanut Noodle Sauce into a bowl and place it next to the rice noodles.

2 Put the carrots, bean sprouts, purple cabbage, roasted cashews, cilantro, scallions, sesame seeds, vegan kimchi, sugar snap peas, and soy sauce into bowls of varying sizes and arrange them around the bowl of rice noodles.

3 Add a few lime wedges to each end of the serving board.

Taco Bowl Tuesday Board

SERVES 4

Fills a 20-inch (50 cm) round board

1 batch Veggie Taco
   Crumbles (page 150)
1 batch Vegan Cheese
   Sauce (page 134)
1 cup (240 g) salsa
½ red onion, diced
1 yellow bell pepper,
   cored and diced
6 cups (180 g) chopped
   romaine
4 corn or flour tortillas,
   warmed
1 cup (16 g) chopped
   cilantro
1 cup (240 g) pico de
   gallo
1 (15-ounce [420 g])
   can pinto beans,
   drained and rinsed
3 scallions, chopped
1 lime, quartered
1 avocado, peeled,
   pitted, and sliced
4 Baked Tortilla Bowls
   (page 135) or store-
   bought tortilla bowls

Taco Tuesday is a weekly tradition in our house. If we aren't eating from a board we're hitting up our local taco truck for takeout. Taco bowls are highly fillable and super customizable, making them perfect for both eager and picky eaters. If you have time, bake your own tortilla bowls for a healthier alternative to the packaged variety. To build a taco bowl, start with a pile of romaine and a spoonful of Veggie Taco Crumbles, made with cauliflower, mushrooms, and a smattering of spices. Add a drizzle of Vegan Cheese Sauce and go wild with the toppings. Warm tortillas offer extra sustenance for the hungrier guests at your dinner table.

1 Scoop the Veggie Taco Crumbles into a medium-size serving bowl and place it in the center of the board. Warm the Vegan Cheese Sauce in a saucepan, then transfer it to a small bowl and place it next to the crumbles.

2 Pour the salsa into a small bowl and place it at the top of the board. Working clockwise, add the red onion, yellow bell pepper, romaine, tortillas, cilantro, pico de gallo, pinto beans, and scallions to the board. Fill in any large gaps with lime wedges.

3 Add the sliced avocado to a small plate and set it off to the side or set it on the board if you have space. Serve with the Baked Tortilla Bowls and your favorite margarita recipe, if desired.

Sunday Night Pasta Board

SERVES 6 TO 8
Fills a 14 x 27-inch (35 x 70 cm) rectangular board

16 ounces (454 g) whole wheat or gluten-free spaghetti

8 ounces (227 g) whole wheat or gluten-free macaroni

Olive oil

1 (24-ounce [672 g]) jar organic marinara sauce

1 batch Vegan Cheese Sauce (page 134)

1 batch Lemony Pea Pesto (page 141)

1 batch Sautéed Mushrooms (page 147)

1 demi ciabatta baguette, sliced, toasted, and rubbed with a cut garlic clove

1 cup (150 g) peas, warmed

1 cup (140 g) sun-dried tomatoes, roughly chopped

2 tablespoons (7 g) red pepper flakes

¼ cup (25 g) vegan Parmesan

1 bunch fresh basil

I thought I loved pasta until I met my husband. Every time we visit my in-laws they prepare a big spaghetti feast with pasta, sauces, and bread lined up in the center of the dining room table. Of course, there's plenty of wine to go around, too. This Sunday Night Pasta Board has a little bit of something for everyone. Marinara, pesto, vegan cheese sauce, sautéed mushrooms, and sun-dried tomatoes offer exciting flavor and texture variations for building a perfect bowl of pasta.

1 Cook the spaghetti and macaroni according to the package directions. Drain, rinse, and toss each batch of pasta with a little swirl of olive oil to prevent the noodles from sticking together.

2 Transfer the cooked spaghetti and macaroni to two loaf pans and place them slightly offset in the center of your serving board.

3 Warm the marinara sauce in a saucepan over low heat. Carefully spoon the sauce into a serving bowl and place it in the upper left corner of the board. Cover until ready to eat.

4 Warm the Vegan Cheese Sauce in a saucepan over low heat. Spoon the sauce into a bowl and place in the lower left corner of the board. Cover until ready to eat.

5 Scoop the Lemony Pea Pesto into a bowl the same size as the cheese sauce and place it in the bottom right corner of the board.

6 Scoop the Sautéed Mushrooms into a small bowl and place near the marinara sauce. Cover until ready to eat. Sprinkle the red pepper flakes into a small bowl and place near the marinara sauce.

7 Cluster the baguette pieces across the board.

8 Pour the peas and sun-dried tomatoes into small bowls and place them on the board.

9 Split the vegan Parmesan between two mini bowls and place one at each end of the board. Tuck fresh basil leaves throughout the board.

Build-Your-Own Sloppy Joes Board

SERVES 4

Fills an 11 x 16-inch (28 x 40 cm) rectangular board

4 whole wheat hamburger buns

1 batch Tempeh Sloppy Joes (page 149)

1 cup (70 g) shredded purple cabbage

1 cup (30 g) shredded romaine lettuce

1 cup (150 g) dill pickle chips

¼ cup (60 ml) ketchup (Primal Kitchen preferred)

1 (15-ounce [420 g]) bag sweet potato fries, baked

1 (8-ounce [227 g]) bag potato chips (optional)

Those familiar with traditional Sloppy Joes know they're not much to look at: a whole lot of brown mush. On this plant-based board, Sloppy Joes get a makeover with the addition of colorful and crunchy vegetables. Top your bottom hamburger bun with a scoop of Tempeh Sloppy Joes filling and pile it high with vibrant purple cabbage and refreshing romaine. It's a tradition in our house to add a few potato chips to the sandwich for extra crunch—just trust me! A batch of sweet potato fries makes this board a complete and satisfying meal.

1 Warm a cast-iron skillet over medium heat and toast the tops and bottoms of the hamburger buns, about a minute on each side. Loosely assemble the buns in a loaf pan and cover with a kitchen towel to keep warm. Set the pan on the right side of the board.

2 Scoop the Tempeh Sloppy Joes filling into a medium bowl and add a spoon. Set it on the left side of the board just next to the buns.

3 Transfer the shredded cabbage and lettuce to bowls of equal size and place at opposite ends of the board.

4 Fill a small bowl with the dill pickle chips and place it in the upper left corner of the board.

5 Fill two mini bowls with ketchup and place in the middle of the board at opposite ends.

6 Fill in gaps on the board with baked sweet potato fries and serve with a bowl of potato chips, if desired.

Cincinnati-Style Chili Dinner Board

SERVES 4 TO 6

Fills a 20-inch (50 cm) round board

1 pound (454 g) spaghetti, cooked al dente

1 teaspoon olive oil

4 Carrot Dogs (page 128) or vegan hot dogs, cooked

4 whole wheat hot dog buns

2 tablespoons (30 ml) yellow mustard

½ cup (80 g) diced yellow onion

1 cup (70 g) oyster crackers

1 (10-ounce [280 g]) bag fresh salad greens

1 batch Basic Balsamic Vinaigrette (page 135)

1 batch Cincinnati-Style Vegan Chili (page 130)

1½ cups (180 g) vegan cheddar-style cheese shreds

Have you heard of Cincinnati-style chili? When I was a kid, a stop at Skyline Chili was essential on each family visit to Ohio and vacation to Florida. Most people are surprised by the unique blend of seasonings at first taste. The original recipe is top secret, but my interpretation includes cocoa, cinnamon, and a dash of vegan Worcestershire sauce. Traditionally, Cincinnati-style chili has no beans, so I kept it that way. Rather, tempeh offers fantastic texture and soaks up the smattering of spices that make this dish so distinct. Cincinnati-style chili is rarely eaten alone. Instead, spoon it over spaghetti or a vegan hot dog and top with vegan cheddar cheese.

1 Drain the spaghetti but don't rinse it. Transfer the pasta to a large serving bowl and toss with a little drizzle of olive oil to prevent the noodles from sticking together. Place the spaghetti on your serving board.

2 Tuck the Carrot Dogs or vegan hot dogs into hot dog buns and line them up on the serving board. Fill a mini bowl with the yellow mustard and place it next to the hot dogs.

3 Fill two small bowls with the yellow onion and oyster crackers. Place the bowls on either side of the vegan hot dogs.

4 Add the fresh salad greens to a large bowl and toss with the Basic Balsamic Vinaigrette.

5 Just before eating, scoop the warm Cincinnati-Style Vegan Chili into a medium bowl and set it on the serving board. Fill a smaller bowl with the vegan cheddar-style cheese shreds and place it next to the chili.

6 To eat, spoon the chili over the spaghetti and vegan hot dogs and top with the cheese, oyster crackers, and diced onion. Serve alongside the salad greens.

Teriyaki Cabbage Wraps Board

SERVES 4 TO 6

Fills a 16 x 24-inch (40 x 60 cm) board or marble pastry slab

½ batch Cauliflower Lentil Balls (page 137)

1½ cups (360 ml) teriyaki sauce, divided

1 head napa cabbage, leaves trimmed and cleaned

1½ cups (180 g) peeled and julienned carrot

1½ cups (105 g) shredded purple cabbage

1 bunch scallions, thinly sliced on the diagonal

1 cup (145 g) roasted cashews

2 tablespoons (30 ml) chili garlic sauce

2 tablespoons (30 ml) soy sauce or coconut aminos

2 tablespoons (16 g) sesame seeds

4 cups (280 g) broccoli florets

2 tablespoons (30 ml) toasted sesame oil

This Asian-inspired meal board is exploding with flavor, color, and texture. Crunchy napa cabbage leaves provide a nutritious and sturdy vessel for teriyaki-drenched Cauliflower Lentil Balls, vibrant vegetables, and savory sauces. The Cauliflower Lentil Balls are gluten-free, soy-free, and nut-free, making this a great meal board to serve to a group with diverse food sensitivities. Just make sure to read the label on your preferred teriyaki sauce and nix the soy sauce and/or cashews if your dinner guests have allergies.

1 Combine the Cauliflower Lentil Balls and 1 cup (240 ml) of the teriyaki sauce in a large skillet and bring to a simmer over low heat. Gently simmer the Cauliflower Lentil Balls until warmed throughout and the teriyaki sauce has thickened slightly, 5 minutes. Cover the skillet to keep the Cauliflower Lentil Balls warm until ready to serve.

2 Set a bowl in the middle of your serving board large enough to hold the Cauliflower Lentil Balls. Place the napa cabbage leaves around the bowl, layering larger leaves on the bottom and smaller leaves on top.

3 Place the carrot, purple cabbage, scallions, and roasted cashews in small bowls. Set two bowls at the bottom of the board and two bowls at the top of the board.

4 Pour the chili garlic sauce, soy sauce, and the remaining ½ cup (120 ml) teriyaki sauce into mini bowls and place them on the left side of the board. Fill a small bowl with the sesame seeds and place it by the sauces.

5 Steam the broccoli, transfer it to a medium bowl, and drizzle with the toasted sesame oil. Place the bowl of steamed broccoli in the upper right corner of your serving board.

6 Transfer the warmed teriyaki Cauliflower Lentil Balls to the bowl in the center of the board and serve immediately.

Grilled Cheese and Roasted Tomato Soup Board

SERVES 4

Fills an 11 x 16-inch (28 x 40 cm) board or a 9 x 13-inch (23 x 33 cm) sheet pan

1 batch Roasted
 Tomato Soup
 with Rosemary
 (page 146)
4 Vegan Grilled
 Cheese Sandwiches
 (page 150)
1 cup (150 g) dill
 pickle chips
12 ounces (336 g)
 cherry tomatoes
Juice of ½ lemon
1 apple
2 cups (100 g) crinkle-
 cut potato chips
6 ounces (168 g) fresh
 salad greens
1 batch Basic Balsamic
 Vinaigrette
 (page 135)

Is there anything more comforting than a grilled cheese sandwich and a warm bowl of homemade tomato soup? It's always been a chilly, rainy day go-to in my house. This Grilled Cheese and Roasted Tomato Soup Board comes together quickly if you meal prep the Vegan Cheese Sauce and Roasted Tomato Soup with Rosemary ahead of time. Both recipes keep well in the fridge for several days. The sweet apple slices, sour dill pickles, and crunchy potato chips on this board pair perfectly with the hearty main course. Serve this board with fresh greens dressed with balsamic vinaigrette or opt for your family's favorite salad.

1 Ladle the Roasted Tomato Soup with Rosemary into four small bowls or one large bowl and place near the middle of the board.

2 Cut the Vegan Grilled Cheese Sandwiches in half. Layer them from the upper and lower left-hand corners of the board in toward the soup.

3 Fill a small bowl with the dill pickle chips and place near the bottom right corner of the board.

4 Add clusters of cherry tomatoes around the tomato soup and at the top of the board.

5 Pour the lemon juice into a bowl. Use an apple slicer to cut the apple into equal wedges and immediately toss them with the lemon juice to prevent browning. Slice each wedge in half lengthwise and add small apple clusters to the top, middle, and bottom of the board.

6 Fill in any gaps on the board with the crinkle-cut potato chips.

7 Fill a bowl with fresh greens and toss with the Basic Balsamic Vinaigrette for serving alongside.

Coconut Chickpea Curry Board

SERVES 6
Fills a 20-inch (50 cm) round board

1 batch Coconut Chickpea
  Curry (page 138)
1 (9-ounce [252 g]) jar
  mango chutney
1 batch Pistachio Cabbage
  Slaw (page 144)
1 cucumber, sliced
4 cups (640 g) cooked
  brown basmati rice
6 pieces naan, warmed
1 batch Spiced Potatoes
  and Cauliflower
  (page 148)

This Coconut Chickpea Curry Board is inspired by Indian ingredients and flavors that run the gamut from spicy to sweet. Coconut Chickpea Curry serves as the main course and calls for Indian curry paste—a red or green Thai curry paste will offer a completely different (but still delicious) result. Spoon the curry over basmati rice and sop up the leftovers with a warm piece of naan. Sliced cucumber and Pistachio Cabbage Slaw refresh the palate, while mango chutney provides sweet relief from the spicy and savory flavors across the board.

1 Set a serving bowl large enough to hold the Coconut Chickpea Curry on the board. You'll scoop the warm curry into the bowl just before serving.

2 Spoon the mango chutney into a small bowl and place it on the board.

3 Set the Pistachio Cabbage Slaw on the left side of the board. Fan the cucumber slices along the edge of the board between the slaw and the curry.

4 Divide the rice between two medium bowls. Set one on the board and one off to the side of the board in case you need extra.

5 Arrange the naan along the left side of the board beneath the slaw.

6 Take the Spiced Potatoes and Cauliflower out of the warm oven and transfer to a medium serving bowl. Place it on the board next to the naan.

7 Just before serving, uncover the curry and spoon it into the serving bowl you set on the board.

Loaded Vegan Chili Board

SERVES 6

Fills a 20-inch (50 cm) round board

1 batch Hearty Pinto
    and Black Bean Chili
    (page 140)
1 bunch scallions,
    thinly sliced
1 jalapeño, seeded and
    diced
1 beefsteak tomato,
    cored and diced
3 medium carrots,
    julienned and cut
    into 2-inch (5 cm)
    pieces
1 cup (150 g) corn,
    cooked
1 (2.25-ounce [63 g])
    can sliced black
    olives
1 avocado, peeled and
    sliced
1 (12-ounce [340 g])
    container vegan sour
    cream or homemade
    vegan sour cream
5 ounces (140 g) baked
    corn tortilla chips
    or grain-free tortilla
    chips
1 lime, quartered

The savory and spicy aroma of chili reminds me of my grandma's house. When I was a kid, she always had a pot simmering on the stove. To this day, I get a warm and cozy feeling whenever I make chili for my family or friends. The Hearty Pinto and Black Bean Chili on this board is free of gluten, soy, and nuts, making it ideal for serving a group with diverse food allergies and sensitivities. Allow your guests to serve themselves and load their steaming bowls of chili with veggies, avocado, and vegan sour cream. Not only are they great for dipping, but tortilla chips also offer a satisfying crunch when crumbled and used as a chili topping.

1 Make the Hearty Pinto and Black Bean Chili. Keep it covered on the stove and reheat gently just before serving.

2 Place a trivet or a large serving bowl on the board as a placeholder for the chili.

3 Scoop the sliced scallions into a small bowl and set it on the board.

4 Place the diced jalapeño in a mini bowl and set it on the board.

5 Scoop the tomato, carrots, and corn into bowls of similar size and place them on the board.

6 Drain the can of olives. Pour the olives into a small bowl and set it on the board.

7 Arrange the avocado slices in clusters across the board.

8 Scoop the vegan sour cream into a bowl and set it on the board.

9 Add handfuls of tortilla chips to the board, filling in any large gaps. Scatter the lime wedges across the board, overlapping the tortilla chips.

10 Transfer the pot of warm chili to the trivet, or ladle the chili into the serving bowl you set on the board as a placeholder.

Rainbow Chopped Salad Board

SERVES 6

Fills a 20-inch (50 cm) round board

8 cups (240 g) chopped
romaine lettuce,
plus more romaine
leaves for serving

2 batches Crispy
Spiced Chickpeas
(page 138)

1 pint (300 g) grape
tomatoes, halved

1 red bell pepper, cored
and chopped

4 carrots, julienned and
chopped

1 yellow bell pepper,
cored and chopped

1 cup (150 g) corn,
warmed

4 scallions, thinly sliced

1 cup (60 g) fresh basil,
chopped

1 cup (150 g) peas,
warmed

1 cup (150 g) fresh
blueberries

2 cups (140 g) chopped
purple cabbage

1 batch Basic Bal-
samic Vinaigrette
(page 135)

I love a chopped salad. When all of the salad components are a similar size, it makes it easy to get a forkful of everything all in one bite. This Rainbow Chopped Salad Board celebrates the gorgeous spectrum of natural plant pigments that give fruits and vegetables their vibrant colors. While most of the salad offerings on this board are raw, Crispy Spiced Chickpeas and warmed corn and peas offer an interesting temperature and texture contrast against the cool, crunchy vegetables. Encourage your dinner companions to fill their bowl with at least one food of each color to complete the rainbow and reap the biggest health benefits.

1 Divide the chopped romaine lettuce among six salad bowls and set off to the side of the board.

2 Remove the leaves from another head of romaine. Rinse the leaves and trim the ends. Cover the board with the romaine leaves, overlapping to blanket the entire board.

3 Transfer the Crispy Spiced Chickpeas to a shallow bowl and set it in the middle of the board.

4 Place the grape tomatoes on the board and set the red bell pepper next to them. Set the carrots next to the bell pepper and continue to arrange the salad components in the order of the rainbow.

5 Serve the chopped salad with the Basic Balsamic Vinaigrette.

CHAPTER 4

Seasonal and Celebration Boards

Game Day Cauliflower
Wings Board
92

Midsummer Backyard
BBQ Board
95

Thanksgiving
Snack Board
96

Oktoberfest
Grazing Board
99

Spring Forward Board
100

Fall Harvest Board
102

Winter Solstice Board
105

New Year's Eve
Champagne Toast
Board
106

Pizza Party Board
108

◂◂ New Year's Eve Champagne
Toast Board (page 106)

Game Day Cauliflower Wings Board

SERVES 6

Fills a 14 x 27-inch (35 x 70 cm) rectangular board

1 batch Classic Buffalo
  Cauliflower Wings
  (page 129)
1 batch Sticky Sesame
  Cauliflower Wings
  (page 129)
1 batch Sweet and
  Spicy Adobo
  Cauliflower Wings
  (page 130)
1 cup (240 ml) vegan
  ranch dressing
1 cup (150 g) dill
  pickle chips
1 cucumber, thinly
  sliced
1 bunch radishes,
  tops trimmed
1 bunch celery,
  trimmed and sliced
  into 4-inch (10 cm)
  sticks
1 pound (454 g)
  carrots, peeled and
  cut into 4-inch
  (10 cm) sticks
1 small pineapple,
  cut into wedges

I've never been much of a sports fan, but you can get me to watch pretty much any game with the promise of a snack buffet. This extra-large board offers a trio of tender, flavorful cauliflower wings and crudités with vegan ranch for dipping. Depending on the size of your cauliflower head, you can expect to make between 75 and 100 wings—plenty for feeding a small group of sports fans. After all of the salty, savory cauliflower wings, fresh pineapple offers sweet relief and a tasty palate cleanser for the next round of hors d'oeuvres.

1 Place three squares of parchment paper or wax paper on the serving board. Pile the Classic Buffalo Cauliflower Wings at the bottom, the Sticky Sesame Cauliflower Wings in the middle, and the Sweet and Spicy Adobo Cauliflower Wings at the top.

2 Pour the vegan ranch dressing into a small bowl and place it in the middle of the board next to the Sticky Sesame Cauliflower Wings. Scoop the pickles into another small bowl and place near the top of the board.

3 Cluster the cucumber slices in groups of four at the bottom, middle, and top of the board. Divide the radishes into three groups and place them next to the cucumbers.

4 Create clusters of celery and carrot sticks and group them around the perimeter of the board. Fill in any gaps on the board with pineapple wedges.

Midsummer Backyard BBQ Board

SERVES 4

Fills a 14 x 27-inch (35 x 70 cm) rectangular board

1 batch Vegan Mac and
Cheese (page 134)

1 pint (300 g)
blueberries

1 pound (454 g)
strawberries

4 whole wheat
hamburger buns

¼ cup (60 ml) ketchup

¼ cup (60 ml) yellow
mustard

1 cup (150 g) dill pickle
chips

4 ears grilled corn

2 cups (60 g) leafy
greens

1 red onion, sliced

4 BBQ Tempeh Burgers
(page 128)

2 tomatoes, sliced

Juice of ½ lemon

1 apple

8 Chocolate-Dipped
Pretzel Sparklers
(page 130)

Fire up the grill and prepare a full-on feast for your Fourth of July celebration or casual summer dinner in the backyard. All the best vegan grillers and sides are here, with a few festive surprises. Chow down on Vegan Mac and Cheese, BBQ Tempeh Burgers with all of the fixings, and, of course, grilled corn. Finish off the meal with a Chocolate-Dipped Pretzel Sparkler (or two) for dessert as you settle in to watch the fireworks.

1 Scoop the Vegan Mac and Cheese into a medium bowl and set toward the bottom of the serving board. Pour the blueberries into a similar-size bowl and place it next to the mac and cheese.

2 Divide the strawberries into equal groups and cluster them in a diagonal line up the serving board.

3 Place a linen napkin inside of a loaf pan and nestle the hamburger buns inside of it. Place the loaf pan on the right side of the board.

4 Squirt the ketchup and mustard into mini bowls and place them next to the mac and cheese. Put the pickle chips in a small bowl and place it next to the ketchup and mustard.

5 Place two ears of grilled corn on the left side of the board near the ketchup and mustard. Place the other two ears of corn at the top of the board.

6 Scatter the leafy greens directly on the board between the two clusters of corn and place the sliced red onion next to it, above the buns.

7 Arrange the BBQ Tempeh Burgers on top of the leafy greens. Place the sliced tomatoes on a small plate to prevent the juices from making the other toppings soggy.

8 Pour the lemon juice into a small bowl. Slice the apple into ¼-inch (6 mm) rounds and press with a small star-shaped cookie cutter. Toss the apple stars in the lemon juice to prevent them from browning and set them on the board next to the strawberry clusters.

9 Divide the Chocolate-Dipped Pretzel Sparklers into three groups and place one near the bottom, one near the middle, and one near the top of the board.

Thanksgiving Snack Board

SERVES 4 TO 6
Fills a 20-inch (50 cm) round board

1 batch Rosemary Mashed
 Potatoes (page 146)

1 batch Sautéed Mush-
 rooms (page 147)

1 demi ciabatta baguette,
 sliced

1 ounce (28 g) vegan butter

1½ cups (225 g) mixed
 olives

1 cup (150 g) dried
 cranberries

1 cup (150 g) candied
 pecans

1 batch Pumpkin-
 Spiced Pumpkin
 Seeds (page 145)

2 tablespoons (30 ml)
 maple syrup

1 head garlic, roasted

2 pears, sliced in half
 lengthwise

Juice of ½ lemon

1 cup (150 g) dried
 apricots

1 pound (454 g) seedless
 red grapes, cut into
 small clusters

1 (5-ounce [140 g]) box
 pita crackers

This Thanksgiving Snack Board reframes the traditional Thanksgiving dinner as a plant-based feast with familiar, comforting flavors in a snackable format. It would be a perfect board to serve the night before Thanksgiving as houseguests trickle in or in place of a large meal if you're having a more intimate and casual holiday.

1 Place the bowl of Rosemary Mashed Potatoes on the board and cover to keep warm until ready to serve.

2 Place the Sautéed Mushrooms on the board next to the mashed potatoes.

3 Layer half of the baguette slices along the right edge of the board and place a mini bowl with vegan butter at the top.

4 Transfer the mixed olives to a small bowl and place it on the other side of the mashed potatoes. Layer the remaining baguette slices along the left edge of the board above the olives.

5 Pour the dried cranberries and candied pecans into bowls of similar size and place them in the center of the board. Transfer the Pumpkin-Spiced Pumpkin Seeds to a pumpkin-shaped bowl and place it in the curve of the baguette slices on the right side of the board.

6 Pour the maple syrup into a mini bowl and set it near the top of the board next to the candied pecans. Place the roasted garlic head directly on the board or in a mini bowl in the curve of the baguette slices on the left side of the board.

7 Place the pear halves at the top, middle, and bottom of the board. Rub the cut sides of the pear with lemon juice to prevent them from browning.

8 Add a handful of dried apricots to the very top of the board.

9 Add half of the grape clusters to the top of the board next to the dried apricots and the remaining grape clusters between the dried cranberries and mushrooms.

10 Layer the pita crackers along the left side of the board and through the middle, filling in any open spaces.

Oktoberfest Grazing Board

SERVES 8
Fills a 14 x 27-inch (35 x 70 cm) rectangular board

1 batch Vegan
  Beer Cheese Dip
  (page 149) or Vegan
  Cheese Sauce
  (page 134)
1 (32-ounce [896 g]) jar
  sauerkraut
1 (8-ounce [227 g]) jar
  German mustard
1 (12.5-ounce [350 g])
  jar mini gherkin
  pickles
2 (14-ounce [392 g])
  packages vegan
  bratwurst
8 bratwurst buns
8 Bavarian pretzels,
  fresh or frozen and
  cooked
Juice of 1 lemon
2 apples

Oktoberfest is an annual two-week festival held in Munich that begins in late September and ends on the first Sunday of October. The fest is marked by large beer halls, music, dancing, and, of course, lots of food. This Oktoberfest Grazing Board offers a taste of the traditional German festival with a plant-based twist. You may be able to find vegan Bavarian pretzels at your local bakery; everything else on this board should be easy to source. Round out the experience with a variety of German and Oktoberfest beers (optional, but recommended).

1 Make the Vegan Beer Cheese Dip or Vegan Cheese Sauce, remove from the heat, and cover the saucepan with a lid.

2 Pour the sauerkraut into a medium serving bowl and place it on the board.

3 Scoop the mustard and mini gherkin pickles into small bowls and place them on the board.

4 Preheat your oven to 350°F (180°C or gas mark 4).

5 Cook the vegan bratwurst according to the package directions. Transfer the bratwurst to a plate and cover to keep warm.

6 Divide the bratwurst buns and Bavarian pretzels between two baking sheets. Place the baking sheets in the preheated oven and warm the buns and pretzels for 3 to 5 minutes.

7 Pour the lemon juice into a bowl. Slice the apples and immediately toss with the lemon juice to prevent them from browning. Layer the apple slices on the board.

8 While the buns and pretzels are in the oven, gently reheat the Vegan Beer Cheese Dip. Transfer the warmed buns and pretzels to the board and place six of the vegan brats in the buns. Slice the remaining two vegan brats into small pieces and set them on the board.

9 Pour the Vegan Beer Cheese Dip into a serving bowl and set it in the middle of the board near the pretzels.

Spring Forward Board

SERVES 6

Fills a 16 x 24-inch (40 x 60 cm) board or marble pastry board

1 head garlic, unpeeled

1½ teaspoons olive oil, plus more for sautéing

1 batch Warm Arugula and Artichoke Dip (page 150)

8 ounces (227 g) asparagus, trimmed

1 batch Edamame Mint Dip (page 139)

12 ounces (340 g) sugar snap peas

2 nectarines, sliced

1 small head broccoli, cut into florets

1 celery heart, trimmed into 3-inch (7.5 cm) sticks

3 kiwi, peeled and sliced

1 bunch radishes, trimmed

1 demi ciabatta baguette, sliced and toasted

1 (4.25-ounce [120 g]) box almond flour crackers

After a long winter of feasting on soups and stews, the arrival of spring brings a colorful crop of fruits and vegetables perfect for snacking. This Spring Forward Board celebrates warmer weather and the desire to eat vibrant, fresh foods once again. Warm Arugula and Artichoke Dip stands in cozy contrast to cool, refreshing Edamame Mint Dip, both of which are perfect with sliced veggies, crackers, and bread.

1 Preheat your oven to 400°F (200°C or gas mark 6). Place the head of garlic on a small square of aluminum foil and drizzle with the olive oil. Fold up the edges and twist the top to secure the garlic in the foil packet and place it on a baking sheet. Roast the garlic for 35 minutes, remove from the oven, and set aside to cool.

2 When the garlic is done, lower the oven temperature to 350°F (180°C or gas mark 4) and bake the Warm Arugula and Artichoke Dip. Lower the oven heat once again to 200°F (100°C or gas mark ½) to keep the dip warm while you assemble the rest of the board.

3 Lightly oil and sauté the asparagus in a cast-iron skillet over medium heat until bright green and tender, about 5 minutes. Transfer the cast-iron skillet to the oven to keep the asparagus warm until ready to serve.

4 Scoop the Edamame Mint Dip into a small serving bowl and set it on the board.

5 Place a cluster of sugar snap peas next to the Edamame Mint Dip and another cluster of peas on the opposite end of the board.

6 Divide the nectarine slices into three groups and place them across the board.

7 Place some of the broccoli florets near each cluster of nectarine slices. Set a small trivet on your serving board and place the Warm Arugula and Artichoke Dip on it. Place the celery next to the dip.

8 Arrange the kiwi slices in three clusters and fan them on the board.

9 Place the radishes around the Edamame Mint Dip. Transfer the roasted garlic to a mini bowl and set it on the board to be squeezed out onto bread or crackers, as desired.

10 Arrange the baguette slices and crackers near each bowl of dip.

11 Just before serving, add the warm asparagus spears to the board.

Fall Harvest Board

SERVES 4 TO 6
Fills an 11 x 16-inch (28 x 40 cm) rectangular board

1 batch Butternut
   Squash Soup Shooters
   (page 136)
1 batch Maple and Date
   Sweet Potato Dip
   (page 142)
1 sleeve vegan graham
   crackers
1 (8-ounce [227 g])
   bag giant Peruvian
   Inca corn
1 (5-ounce [140 g])
   package dried and
   sweetened orange
   slices
2 Belgian endive, one
   red and one white,
   leaves pulled apart
1 (16-ounce [454 g])
   bag petite carrots
8 ounces (227 g)
   champagne grapes
1 Granny Smith apple
1 Pink Lady apple
Juice of 1 lemon
1 cup (150 g) green grapes
Eucalyptus leaves, for
   decoration (optional)

This Fall Harvest Board celebrates the bounty of fruits and vegetables that come with cooler weather. You'll find the usual suspects—butternut squash and apple—as well as a few surprises like crunchy Belgian endive and delicate champagne grapes. Soup shooters are always a conversation starter and a great way to add a warm, cozy feel to an autumn snack spread.

1   Place eight 2-ounce (60 ml) shot glasses in groups of two or three across the board. Make the soup and keep it warm on the stove.

2   Set the bowl of Maple and Sweet Potato Dip on the right side of the board just above the cluster of soup shooters. Fan the graham crackers around the left side of the bowl.

3   Pour the giant Peruvian Inca corn into a bowl and place it toward the lower left corner of the board. Fan the dried orange slices along the lower left corner of the board around the bowl.

4   Place the Belgian endive leaves on the left side of the board just above the bowl of giant Peruvian Inca corn.

5   Stack the petite carrots in the upper left corner of the board pointing in toward the middle of the board.

6   Place a cluster of champagne grapes in the upper right corner of the board, in the middle of the board, and in the bottom right corner of the board.

7   Core and cut the apples into thin slices and immediately brush them with lemon juice to prevent browning.

8   Place a stack of Granny Smith apple slices at the very top of the board and at the bottom of the board below the soup shooters.

9   Place the Pink Lady apple slices on the right side of the board above the Maple and Date Sweet Potato Dip and on the left side of the board between the carrots and the endive.

10 Fill in any gaps on the board with green grapes. Tuck in a few eucalyptus leaves for added decorative flair, if you'd like.

11 Just before serving, pour the soup into the shot glasses. Please be careful; the soup should be warm, but not hot.

Winter Solstice Board

SERVES 6
Fills a 20-inch (50 cm) round board

1 batch Caramelized
   Onion Dip (page 136)
2 pomegranates
1 blood orange, sliced
   into wedges
1 grapefruit, sliced into
   wedges
1 navel orange, sliced into
   wedges
3 clementines, cut in half
   crosswise
1 delicata squash
½ tablespoon (7.5 ml)
   olive oil
¼ teaspoon salt
Several twists of black
   pepper
1 demi ciabatta baguette,
   sliced
1 batch Miso Roasted
   Brussels Sprouts
   (page 143)
1 (4.25-ounce [120 g]) box
   rosemary and sea salt
   almond flour crackers
8 ounces (225 g) petite
   carrots, sliced in half
   lengthwise
4 or 5 sprigs fresh
   rosemary

It wouldn't be the holiday season without indulgent snacks and sweets. While there's certainly a time and place for treats, there's a lot of produce to celebrate this time of year as well. And, let's be honest, we could all use a reminder to eat our fruits and vegetables in the midst of the holiday craziness. This Winter Solstice Board is a departure from typical holiday party food. From fresh pomegranate and juicy citrus to tender roasted veggies, this seasonal snack board lets your guests enjoy a range of colors, textures, and flavors.

1 Scoop the Caramelized Onion Dip into a bowl, cover, and refrigerate until ready to serve.

2 Remove the arils from one of the pomegranates and pour them into a small bowl. Slice the other pomegranate in half. Place the bowl of pomegranate arils and halved pomegranate on the board.

3 Place the blood orange, grapefruit, and navel orange wedges across the board. Add the clementine halves to the board.

4 Preheat your oven to 425°F (220°C or gas mark 7) and line two baking sheets with parchment paper.

5 Scrub the delicata squash clean and slice in half lengthwise. The skin is edible, so there's no need to peel. Scoop out the seeds and slice each squash half into ½-inch (1.3 cm) half-moons. Transfer the delicata squash to one of the prepared baking sheets, drizzle with the olive oil, sprinkle with the salt and black pepper, and toss to coat. Set aside.

6 Place the delicata squash in the oven and roast for 20 minutes, flipping the pieces halfway through.

7 Transfer the delicata squash to a plate and cover to keep warm.

8 Turn off the oven. Place the baguette slices on one of the baking sheets and put it in the oven. Toast the bread for 3 to 5 minutes, until light golden.

9 Transfer the Miso Roasted Brussels Sprouts, roasted delicata squash, and Caramelized Onion Dip to the serving board. Arrange the crackers around the dip and place clusters of petite carrots and toasted baguette across the board.

10 Tuck fresh rosemary springs throughout the board for garnish.

New Year's Eve Champagne Toast Board

SERVES 6

Fills a 16 x 24-inch (40 x 60 cm) board or marble pastry board

1 (750 ml) bottle brut champagne

2 cups (480 ml) pomegranate juice

1 cup (140 g) pomegranate arils

1 batch Frosted Cranberries (page 139)

1 pint (300 g) raspberries

1 pint (300 g) blackberries

1 pound (454 g) strawberries, halved

1 orange, sliced into wedges

1 bunch fresh rosemary

1 bunch fresh thyme

There aren't many occasions that call for a champagne board, but New Year's Eve is definitely one of them. This New Year's Eve Champagne Toast Board offers the opportunity to impress your guests with more than a fancy bottle of bubbly. Using the berries, pomegranate, orange, and herbs, everyone can spruce up their first sip of the New Year just how they'd like. I recommend setting an alarm for 11:30 p.m. so you don't forget to bring out the board. Allow your guests to mingle, enjoy a snack, and garnish their glasses before popping the champagne at midnight. For a nonalcoholic board, simply swap in sparkling apple cider for the champagne.

1 Place the champagne in an ice bucket filled halfway with ice cubes off to the side of the board to chill until midnight.

2 Set the champagne glasses in the center of the board.

3 Pour the pomegranate juice into a glass carafe and place it at the top of the board.

4 Place the pomegranate seeds in a small bowl and set it near the pomegranate juice.

5 Pour the Frosted Cranberries into a small bowl and set it on the board.

6 Scatter clusters of raspberries, blackberries, and strawberries across the board. Fill in any gaps with orange slices.

7 Tuck fresh rosemary and thyme sprigs throughout the board for garnish.

Pizza Party Board

SERVES 12

Fills a 20-inch (50 cm) round board

1 batch Pizza Dough
  Garlic Knots (page 144)
1 batch Cauliflower Lentil
  Balls (page 137)
1 batch Sautéed
  Mushrooms (page 147)
1 (12-ounce [340 g]) bag
  cauliflower gnocchi
1 (24-ounce [672 g]) jar
  organic marinara sauce
  or 3 cups (720 ml)
  homemade marinara
  sauce, warmed
1 (6-ounce [168 g]) can
  large black olives,
  drained
½ cup (50 g) vegan
  Parmesan
1 green bell pepper,
  cored and sliced
1 yellow bell pepper,
  cored and sliced
1 medium pineapple
1 (4-ounce [112 g])
  package vegan
  pepperoni
6 pepperoncini peppers
6 slices of vegan cheese,
  cut into squares
1 bunch fresh basil

This Pizza Party Board is stuffed with pizzeria snacks and appetizers. A warm bowl of marinara sauce sits in the middle of the board and invites diners to dunk freshly baked Pizza Dough Garlic Knots and Cauliflower Lentil Balls. I like to serve the marinara sauce in a fondue pot and keep it warm over a tealight candle. Mushrooms, olives, pineapple, and vegan pepperoni offer smaller bites in a range of textures and flavors to keep things exciting.

1 Preheat the oven to 200°F (100°C or gas mark ½). Put the Pizza Dough Garlic Knots and Cauliflower Lentil Balls on a large baking sheet and cover with foil. Place the baking sheet in the oven to keep the food warm until you're ready to serve. Transfer the Sautéed Mushrooms to an oven-safe serving bowl. Place it in the warm oven.

2 Make the cauliflower gnocchi according to the package directions. Transfer to an oven-safe serving bowl and place it in the oven to keep warm.

3 Pour the marinara sauce into a serving bowl or fondue pot, set it in the middle of the board, and cover to keep warm. Place two small trivets on the board as placeholders for the Sautéed Mushrooms and cauliflower gnocchi.

4 Pour the olives into a small bowl and set it on the board. Pour the vegan Parmesan into a small bowl and set it on the board.

5 Place the green bell pepper and yellow bell pepper on the board.

6 Slice the pineapple in half lengthwise and scoop out the inside of one half, leaving a ½-inch (13 mm) border all the way around to create a bowl. Dice the other half of the pineapple and transfer the pieces to the pineapple bowl. Set the pineapple on the board.

7 Place the pepperoncini peppers near the vegan Parmesan. Turn off the oven. Place the Pizza Dough Garlic Knots and Cauliflower Lentil Balls directly on the board.

8 Set the bowls of Sautéed Mushrooms and cauliflower gnocchi on top of their respective trivets.

9 Layer the vegan cheese slices at the bottom of the board near the olives and cauliflower gnocchi. Layer the vegan pepperoni slices on the board.

10 Fill in any gaps on the board with fresh basil. Serve with fondue forks for dipping Pizza Dough Garlic Knots, Cauliflower Lentil Balls, and cauliflower gnocchi in the marinara sauce.

CHAPTER 5

Fruit and Dessert Boards

Mini Berry Pie Board
112

Frozen Banana Pops
Board
115

Chocolate Fondue
Board
116

Watermelon Pizza
Board
118

Winter Yogurt Waffle
Bowls Board
121

Mini Bundt Cakes Board
123

Ice Cream Sundae
Board
124

Hot Chocolate
Dessert Boards
126

◀◀ Mini Banana Bundt Cake, Mini Bundt
Cakes Board (page 123)

Mini Berry Pie Board

SERVES 12

Fills an 11 x 16-inch (28 x 40 cm) rectangular board

12 Mini Pie Crusts
(page 131)

1 batch Blueberry
Chia Pie Filling
(page 133)

1 batch Strawberry
Chia Pie Filling
(page 134)

2 ounces (56 g) coconut whipped cream

10 ounces (280 g)
fresh strawberries,
halved or quartered

1 pint (300 g) fresh
blueberries

1 small bunch
fresh mint

1 small bunch
fresh basil

These build-your-own mini pies offer a fun alternative to slice-and-serve desserts. Take a crust, choose your filling (or mix them), and top with coconut whipped cream and fresh berries. Mini pies are just the right size for satisfying your sweet tooth after a filling meal. Too stuffed? The pie filling keeps in the refrigerator for several days and can also be spooned over oatmeal or pancakes for breakfast.

1 Stack the Mini Pie Crusts in groups of two and line them up down the middle of your serving board.

2 Scoop the Blueberry Chia Pie Filling and Strawberry Chia Pie Filling into small bowls and place them on either side of the pie crusts.

3 Fill two mini bowls with coconut whipped cream and place them at opposite ends of the board.

4 Divide the strawberries into three groups and cluster them at the top, middle, and bottom of the board. Use the blueberries to fill in the rest of the board and garnish with a few sprigs of fresh mint and fresh basil.

Frozen Banana Pops Board

SERVES 8
Fills an 11 x 16-inch (28 x 40 cm) rectangular board

4 bananas

1¼ cups (220 g) semisweet vegan chocolate chunks

1 tablespoon (15 ml) refined coconut oil, melted

½ cup (120 g) peanut butter

¼ cup (35 g) pistachios, finely chopped

¼ cup (35 g) almonds, finely chopped

¼ cup (35 g) vegan sprinkles

¼ cup (5 g) freeze-dried strawberries, crushed

¼ cup (20 g) unsweetened shredded coconut

½ cup (20 g) potato chips, crushed

½ cup (70 g) pretzels, crushed

2 tablespoons (30 g) flaky sea salt

This Frozen Banana Pops Board takes the humble banana and turns it into a wonderfully creamy, dairy-free treat on a stick. Just slice the bananas in half, stick a Popsicle stick through each, and freeze while you prep the chocolate coating and toppings. Tip: It takes about 2 hours for the banana halves to freeze completely. A few minutes of thawing at room temperature yields a perfect ice cream bar consistency. The chocolate coating hardens quickly after making contact with the frozen banana, so advise your guests to select their toppings before dipping.

1   Line a baking sheet with parchment paper. Peel the bananas and slice them in half crosswise. Stick a Popsicle stick through the thicker end of each banana and push it halfway through. Arrange the bananas in a single layer on the baking sheet and freeze for at least 2 hours.

2   Meanwhile, make the chocolate coating. Pour the chocolate chunks and coconut oil into a glass bowl and microwave in 30-second intervals until melted. Alternatively, you can melt the chocolate chunks using a double boiler. Pour the chocolate coating into a small bowl and set aside.

3   Set a square of parchment paper on the board. Put the peanut butter, pistachios, almonds, vegan sprinkles, freeze-dried strawberries, shredded coconut, crushed potato chips, and crushed pretzels in bowls of similar size. Pour the flaky sea salt into a mini bowl. Set all of the toppings around the perimeter of the board.

4   Place the bowl of chocolate sauce in the middle and set the frozen banana pops on either side.

5   Have your guests combine their chosen toppings in a small bowl before selecting their banana pop; each banana pop holds about 2 tablespoons (16 g) of toppings.

6   The chocolate coating will harden very quickly when it comes into contact with the frozen banana. Allow everyone to dip their bananas in the chocolate coating and quickly sprinkle with their selected toppings.

Chocolate Fondue Board

SERVES 4

Fills a 14-inch (35 cm) round board with a lip

1 (10-ounce [280 g])
    bag vegan
    marshmallows
8 ounces (227 g) fresh
    strawberries
6 ounces (168 g) fresh
    raspberries
6 ounces (168 g) fresh
    blackberries
4 clementines, peeled
    and segments pulled
    apart
1 cup (140 g) pretzels
1 cup (80 g) potato
    chips
1 batch Vegan Choco-
    late Sauce (page 149)
Juice of ½ lemon
1 apple

One of the few things I inherited from my grandma was her fondue set. Every time I pull it out I imagine the types of parties she and my grandpa hosted for their friends back in the 1960s and 1970s. The best type of fondue pot for chocolate is a smaller pot set over a tealight candle. Even with a small flame, you'll want to stir the chocolate sauce frequently to prevent it from getting too hot. Serve with a variety of sweet, salty, and crunchy dippers for the ultimate chocolate lovers' dessert. If you'd like to scale this recipe up or down, estimate about ¼ cup (60 ml) vegan chocolate sauce and 20 to 25 dippers per person.

1 Set your fondue pot or a small ramekin in the middle of your board.

2 Divide the vegan marshmallows into two clusters and place them on the board. Set the strawberries, raspberries, and blackberries on the board.

3 Add clusters of clementine segments to the board.

4 Pour the pretzels and potato chips onto the board.

5 Transfer the Vegan Chocolate Sauce to your fondue pot or serving bowl and set it on the board.

6 Pour the lemon juice into a bowl. Slice the apple and immediately toss the pieces with the lemon juice to keep them from browning. Layer the apple pieces on the serving board.

7 Serve with fondue forks for dipping.

Watermelon Pizza Board

SERVES 8

Fills a 20-inch (50 cm) round board

1 batch of Strawberry
  Cashew Cheesecake
  Dip (page 133)
¼ cup (60 ml) plain
  vegan cream cheese
1 large seedless
  watermelon
½ teaspoon sea salt
1 sleeve vegan graham
  crackers, broken
1 ounce (28 g) flaky sea
  salt
1 ounce (28 g) chili lime
  seasoning, like Tajín
½ cup (40 g) unsweet-
  ened shredded
  coconut
1 cup (235 ml) coconut
  whipped cream
1 pint (300 g) fresh
  blueberries
6 ounces (168 g) fresh
  raspberries
1½ cups (233 g) fresh
  pineapple, diced
3 kiwi, peeled and cut
  into small triangles
6 ounces (168 g) fresh
  blackberries
2 peaches, diced
1 bunch fresh mint

If you're as amazed by the versatility of watermelon as I am, wait until you make this Watermelon Pizza Board. It makes a perfect summer dessert whether you're hosting a barbecue, pool party, or birthday bash. A thick cross section of watermelon functions perfectly as a pizza "crust," while Strawberry Cashew Cheesecake Dip provides a tasty, creamy base for piling on more fruit. You can preassemble, slice, and serve this watermelon pizza or allow your guests to add their own "sauce" and toppings. Lightly salting and pressing the watermelon will help prevent sogginess from spoiling the fun.

1 Scoop the Strawberry Cashew Cheesecake Dip into a bowl. Mix the vegan cream cheese into the dip and refrigerate until thickened, about 1 hour.

2 Slice the watermelon in half at its largest point, then slice it again to create a 1½-inch (3.8 cm)-thick slab.

3 Lightly rub both sides of the watermelon slab with ¼ teaspoon of salt. Set the watermelon between two kitchen towels for 10 minutes to absorb excess liquid.

4 Set the watermelon on a cutting board and slice into 8 triangles.

5 Carefully transfer the watermelon slices to a round plate or platter and set it in the center of your board along with the Strawberry Cashew Cheesecake Dip. Set the graham cracker squares in two places on opposite sides of the board.

6 Set two mini bowls on the board. Fill one with flaky sea salt and the other with chili lime seasoning. Set two slightly larger bowls on the board and fill with shredded coconut and coconut whipped cream.

7 Arrange the blueberries, raspberries, pineapple, kiwi, blackberries, and peaches on the board around the watermelon.

8 Tuck fresh mint leaves throughout the board for garnish.

Winter Yogurt Waffle Bowls Board

SERVES 4

Fills an 11 x 16-inch (28 x 40 cm) rectangular board or a 9 x 13-inch (23 x 33 cm) sheet pan

2 (5-ounce [140 g]) containers dairy-free vanilla yogurt

2 (5-ounce [140 g]) containers dairy-free strawberry yogurt

2 (5-ounce [140 g]) containers dairy-free mango yogurt

¼ cup (60 ml) maple syrup

½ cup (85 g) vegan mini chocolate chips

6 vegan waffle bowls or cones

1 cup (150 g) granola

½ cup (70 g) pomegranate arils

¼ cup (35 g) sliced almonds

1 orange, peeled and sliced into rounds

½ cup (70 g) raw pistachios

Juice of ½ lemon

1 apple

Fresh rosemary sprigs

This Winter Yogurt Waffle Bowls Board straddles a fine line between indulgent breakfast and dessert. Choose your own adventure! Your family and friends will enjoy mixing and matching three different flavors of dairy-free yogurt and topping it with a variety of seasonal ingredients. Pomegranate arils and orange lend vibrant color and juicy flavor, while nuts and vegan chocolate chips offer a pleasant, contrasting crunch.

1 Scoop the yogurts into three bowls of similar size and place them in a cluster toward the top left of the board.

2 Pour the maple syrup into a mini bowl and the mini chocolate chips into a 4-ounce (120 ml) mason jar and place them in the upper left corner of the board.

3 Stack four of the waffle bowls in the upper right corner of the board. Break the other two into pieces and set aside. Place the granola in the lower left corner of the board.

4 Pour the pomegranate arils and sliced almonds into small bowls of equal size and place them in the middle of the board.

5 Place a small plate in the lower right corner of the board and arrange the orange slices in an overlapping pile.

6 Fill a small bowl with pistachios and place it on the right side of the board.

7 Pour the lemon juice into a bowl. Use an apple slicer to slice the apple into wedges. Then transfer the apple slices to a cutting board and cut each wedge in half lengthwise. Immediately place the apple pieces in the bowl of lemon juice and coat all sides to prevent browning.

8 Add a cluster of apple slices at the top of the board between the yogurt and the waffle bowls and two more clusters on the right side of the board, sandwiching the pistachios.

9 Fill in any gaps on the board with broken waffle bowl pieces and garnish with fresh rosemary.

Mini Bundt Cakes Board

SERVES 6

Fills an 11 x 16-inch (28 x 40 cm) rectangular board

1 batch Mini Banana
  Bundt Cakes
  (page 142)
1 batch Vanilla Glaze
  (page 143)
1 batch Vegan Chocolate
  Sauce (page 149)
1 cup (240 g) creamy
  salted peanut butter
6 ounces (168 g) fresh
  raspberries
6 ounces (168 g) fresh
  blackberries
8 ounces (227 g) fresh
  strawberries, quartered
1 cup (145 g) walnuts,
  finely chopped
1 cup (175 g) mini vegan
  chocolate chips
1 (15-ounce [420 g]) can
  coconut whipped
  cream

Single-serving sweets are always a hit on dessert boards and these mini Bundt cakes are no exception. The distinctive shape of the Bundt cakes, with their decorative sides and hollow centers, is an immediate attention grabber and conversation starter. Serve with a selection of glazes and toppings and you have a showstopper of a dessert board perfect for an engagement party, baby shower, or intimate wedding celebration. This Mini Bundt Cakes Board offers six small Bundt cakes, though each dessert can satisfy two people if enjoyed after a larger meal. The Mini Banana Bundt Cakes can be made ahead of time, but the glaze and chocolate sauce are best enjoyed right away.

1 Make the Mini Banana Bundt Cakes and cool to room temperature. Set the mini Bundt cakes in the center of the board.

2 Pour the Vanilla Glaze and Vegan Chocolate Sauce into small bowls and set them on the board.

3 Scoop the peanut butter into a small bowl and set it on the board.

4 Place clusters of raspberries, blackberries, and strawberries across the board.

5 Pour the walnuts and mini vegan chocolate chips into bowls of similar size and set them on the board.

6 Serve with coconut whipped cream.

Ice Cream Sundae Board

SERVES 8

Fills a 16 x 24-inch (40 x 60 cm) board or marble pastry board

1 batch Vegan Chocolate
Sauce (page 149)

1 pint (480 g) vegan
strawberry ice
cream, homemade or
store-bought

1 pint (480 g) vegan
vanilla ice cream,
homemade or
store-bought

1 pint (480 g) vegan
chocolate ice cream,
homemade or
store-bought

8 Oreo cookies, crushed

1 cup (140 g) pretzels,
crushed

2 yellow peaches, pitted
and diced

½ cup (70 g) roasted and
salted peanuts, finely
chopped

½ cup (70 g) vegan
sprinkles

½ cup (60 g) mini vegan
chocolate chips

½ cup (40 g) unsweetened
shredded coconut

4 vegan graham crackers,
crushed

1 (15-ounce [420 g]) can
coconut whipped cream

Vegan ice cream has come a long way in recent years. It's sweet, creamy, and cool—everything ice cream should be—with none of the dairy. I've found that the creamiest vegan ice creams are made with a coconut cream and cashew base. You can also find vegan ice cream made with almond milk and oat milk. Look for a short, simple ingredient list on the vegan ice cream you choose. Or, better yet, make your own at home. Serve your favorite flavors chilled in an ice bucket alongside Vegan Chocolate Sauce and a selection of sweet, salty, and crunchy toppings.

1 Pour the Vegan Chocolate Sauce into a small bowl. Set aside.

2 Fill a tray or shallow bucket with ice cubes. Put the vegan ice cream containers in the ice so they stay cold. Place the bucket in the center of the board.

3 Place the crushed cookies, crushed pretzels, diced peaches, roasted peanuts, sprinkles, mini vegan chocolate chips, shredded coconut, and crushed graham crackers in small bowls and set them on the board around the ice cream.

4 Serve with coconut whipped cream and small dessert bowls.

Hot Chocolate Dessert Board

SERVES 4
Fills a 20-inch (50 cm) round board

1 batch Salted Hot
  Chocolate
  (page 147)
½ cup (40 g)
  unsweetened
  shredded coconut
4 vegan candy canes,
  crushed, plus more
  for decorating the
  board
1 cup (100 g) coconut
  whipped cream
1 (5-ounce [140 g])
  bag sweet and spicy
  pecans
2 tablespoons (30 g)
  flaky sea salt
10 Oreo cookies
4 mandarin oranges,
  halved
1 (10-ounce [280 g])
  bag mini vegan
  marshmallows
4 cinnamon sticks
Fresh rosemary sprigs
  or winter greenery,
  for decorating
Peppermint schnapps
  or spiced rum
  (optional)

There are few things as cozy and indulgent as sipping a warm mug of hot chocolate. This Hot Chocolate Dessert Board features homemade Salted Hot Chocolate and all of the toppings and treats your guests could possibly want to go along with it. Experiment with adding a few drops of peppermint or orange extract to the hot chocolate for a subtle hint of flavor. Or, if you're serving a group of adults, offer your guests a splash of spiced rum in their mug and make it a boozy hot chocolate board. The spicy pecans may seem like a surprising addition, but they offer just enough heat and contrast nicely with the sweet chocolate and treats.

1 Pour the Salted Hot Chocolate into a thermal carafe to keep warm.

2 Set four mugs along the right side of the board.

3 Fill four small bowls of similar size with shredded coconut, crushed candy canes, coconut whipped cream, and sweet and spicy pecans.

4 Place a mini bowl on the board and fill it with the flaky sea salt.

5 Layer the Oreo cookies on the left side of the serving board.

6 Place the orange halves on the board cut-side up.

7 Pour the mini vegan marshmallows directly onto the board, filling in any gaps between the mugs and bowls.

8 Place the cinnamon sticks at the top of the board. Tuck fresh rosemary or winter greenery in any open spots for decoration.

The Recipes

BBQ Tempeh Burgers

Makes 4

2 (8-ounce [227 g]) packages organic tempeh
½ cup (120 ml) BBQ sauce
1 tablespoon (15 ml) avocado oil
4 whole wheat hamburger buns
Lettuce, tomato, sliced onion, and pickles, for topping

1 Slice the tempeh blocks in half and square off the ends.

2 Arrange the tempeh patties in a single layer in a steamer basket. Place the steamer basket in a skillet filled with 1 inch (2.5 cm) or so of water. Bring the water to a boil, cover the skillet, and reduce the heat to low. Steam the tempeh for 10 minutes. Transfer the tempeh to a plate lined with paper towels and pat dry.

3 Pour the BBQ sauce into a shallow dish and add the tempeh patties. Brush some of the BBQ sauce over the top of the patties, cover, and refrigerate for at least 2 hours. Flip the tempeh patties occasionally so they soak up as much flavor as possible.

4 If using a grill, lightly oil the grate and preheat to medium heat. If using a cast-iron skillet, preheat it and then add the avocado oil. Swirl to coat the bottom of the skillet.

5 When the grill or cast-iron skillet is hot, add the marinated tempeh patties, leaving excess BBQ sauce in the dish. Cook for 5 to 7 minutes on each side, until slightly crisp and browned in spots. Transfer to a plate to cool and brush with leftover BBQ sauce if desired.

6 Serve the BBQ Tempeh Burgers on the Midsummer Backyard BBQ Board (page 95).

Carrot Dogs

NUT-FREE | *Makes 6*

3½ tablespoons (53 ml) low-sodium
   soy sauce, divided
6 medium carrots (about 1 inch [2.5 cm] diameter),
   peeled and ends trimmed
2 tablespoons (30 ml) olive oil
½ teaspoon liquid smoke
1 teaspoon Dijon mustard
½ teaspoon paprika
1 tablespoon (15 ml) maple syrup

1 Bring a pot of water to a boil over medium-high heat and stir in 2 tablespoons (30 ml) of the low-sodium soy sauce. Place the carrots in the water and boil for 12 to 15 minutes, until the carrots are just barely fork tender. Do not overcook. Transfer the carrots to a bowl of ice water to stop the cooking.

2 Combine the remaining 1½ tablespoons (23 ml) soy sauce, olive oil, liquid smoke, Dijon mustard, paprika, and maple syrup in a zip-top silicone bag or loaf pan and shake to combine.

3 Pat the carrots dry and add them to the bag with the marinade. Place the carrots in the fridge to marinate overnight, or for at least 8 hours. Flip the carrots occasionally to coat all sides.

4 When ready to eat, preheat a cast-iron skillet or grill to medium heat. Shake excess marinade from the carrots and place them directly on the skillet or grill. Cook the carrots for 7 to 10 minutes, turning occasionally, until lightly browned on all sides.

5 Serve the Carrot Dogs immediately on the Backyard Campfire Board (page 60), Midsummer Backyard BBQ Board (page 95), or Cincinnati-Style Chili Dinner Board (page 78).

Cauliflower Wings

NUT-FREE, SOY-FREE
Makes about 75 cauliflower wings

1¼ cups (150 g) whole wheat flour
¼ teaspoon garlic powder
¼ teaspoon salt
Few twists of black pepper
1½ cups (360 ml) oat milk
1 large head cauliflower, chopped into florets

1 Preheat the oven to 375°F (190°C or gas mark 5) and line two baking sheets with parchment paper.

2 Combine the whole wheat flour, garlic powder, salt, and black pepper in a very large bowl. Whisk in the oat milk until fully combined; the mixture should be the consistency of pancake batter.

3 Add the cauliflower florets to the bowl and use a rubber spatula to mix and gently coat each piece in the batter.

4 Shake excess batter from each piece of cauliflower as you place the florets in a single layer on the prepared baking sheets. Bake the cauliflower wings for 15 minutes, until golden brown. Remove the wings from the oven, but leave the oven on.

5 Transfer a third of the cauliflower wings to a large mixing bowl and pour in one of the wing sauces (recipes follow). Stir and coat the cauliflower wings in the sauce.

6 Use a slotted spoon to transfer each piece of cauliflower back to the baking sheet, leaving excess sauce behind in the bowl. Reserve the sauce for later.

7 Wipe out the mixing bowl and repeat with the remaining cauliflower wings and sauces.

8 Return the sauced cauliflower wings to the oven and bake for 5 minutes more. Remove the wings from the oven and brush each wing with extra sauce.

9 Serve the cauliflower wings on the Game Day Cauliflower Wings Board (page 92).

Sticky Sesame Garlic Sauce

NUT-FREE

¼ cup (60 ml) sesame oil
1 tablespoon (15 ml) low-sodium soy sauce
1 tablespoon (15 ml) lime juice
2 cloves garlic, minced
1 tablespoon (15 ml) maple syrup
1 teaspoon tapioca flour
1 teaspoon sesame seeds, for serving
1 scallion (dark green part only), thinly sliced, for serving

1 Combine the sesame oil, soy sauce, lime juice, garlic, and maple syrup in a small saucepan. Bring to a gentle simmer over low heat, then stir in the tapioca flour.

2 Continue to stir until the sauce thickens, about 5 minutes. Remove from the heat and toss with a third of the cauliflower wings. Bake the wings as directed at left.

3 Just before serving, sprinkle the cauliflower wings with the sesame seeds and sliced scallion.

Classic Buffalo Sauce

NUT-FREE, SOY-FREE

⅓ cup (80 ml) hot sauce
¼ cup (60 ml) olive oil
½ teaspoon vegan Worcestershire sauce
½ teaspoon maple syrup

1 Combine the hot sauce, olive oil, vegan Worcestershire sauce, and maple syrup in a small saucepan. Bring to a gentle simmer over medium-low heat.

2 Continue to simmer for 5 to 10 minutes, until the sauce reduces and thickens slightly. Remove from the heat and toss with a third of the cauliflower wings. Bake the wings as directed at left.

Sweet and Spicy Adobo Sauce

NUT-FREE, SOY-FREE

1 tablespoon (15 ml) olive oil
2 to 3 tablespoons (30 to 45 ml) sauce from
   a can of chipotle peppers in adobo sauce
1 teaspoon chili powder
2 tablespoons (30 ml) maple syrup
Pinch of salt

1 Combine the olive oil, adobo sauce, chili powder, maple syrup, and salt in a small bowl and whisk to combine.

2 Toss with a third of the cauliflower wings. Bake the wings as directed on page 129.

Chocolate-Dipped Pretzel Sparklers

SOY-FREE | *Makes 24*

1 cup (175 g) semisweet vegan chocolate chips
1½ teaspoons coconut oil
1 cup (140 g) vegan red, white, and blue sprinkles
⅓ cup (95 g) slivered almonds, finely chopped
24 pretzel rods

1 Use a double boiler to melt the chocolate chips. If you don't have a double boiler, you can make your own by setting a heat-safe bowl over a saucepan of simmering water. Add the coconut oil to the chocolate chips and whisk until the chocolate chips have completely melted. Remove from the heat.

2 Line two baking sheets with parchment paper or wax paper. Combine the sprinkles and almonds on a large plate and set it near the stove.

3 Working one at a time, spoon the melted chocolate over the pretzel rods, leaving the bottom third of each pretzel rod bare.

4 Coat the chocolate-covered portion of each pretzel rod with the sprinkles and almonds and carefully place on the prepared baking sheets in a single layer.

5 Chill the chocolate-covered pretzels in the fridge for at least 30 minutes or in the freezer for at least 20 minutes, until the chocolate is dry and firm.

6 Transfer the Chocolate-Dipped Pretzel Sparklers to an airtight container and store in the fridge until ready to serve on the Midsummer Backyard BBQ Board (page 95).

Cincinnati-Style Vegan Chili

Serves 6

2 (8-ounce [227 g]) blocks tempeh
1 tablespoon (15 ml) olive oil
1 cup (160 g) finely chopped yellow onion
5 cloves garlic, minced
2 cups (480 ml) vegetable broth
1 cup (240 ml) tomato sauce
3 tablespoons (45 ml) low-sodium soy sauce
1 teaspoon vegan Worcestershire sauce
1 teaspoon rice vinegar
¼ cup (30 g) unsweetened cocoa powder
1 tablespoon (8 g) ground cinnamon
2 tablespoons (16 g) chili powder
1 teaspoon salt
Pinch of cayenne (optional)

1 Slice the tempeh into 1-inch (2.5 cm)-wide strips and arrange in a large skillet. Fill the skillet with ½ inch (1.3 cm) of water and bring to a simmer over medium-low heat. Cover and cook for 10 minutes.

2 Use a slotted spoon to transfer the tempeh to a cutting board. Pat dry with a clean kitchen towel. Place the tempeh in the bowl of a food processor and pulse just a couple of times until the tempeh is finely chopped. Don't overdo it!

3 Warm the olive oil in a stockpot over medium-low heat. Add the onion and sauté until very soft, about 5 minutes. Add the tempeh and garlic and cook for 5 minutes more.

4 Add the vegetable broth, tomato sauce, soy sauce, vegan Worcestershire sauce, rice vinegar, cocoa powder, cinnamon, chili powder, salt, and cayenne (if using) and stir to combine.

5 Bring the chili to a simmer over medium heat, then cover the pot and turn the heat to low. Continue to cook, covered, for 30 minutes.

6 Serve on the Cincinnati-Style Chili Dinner Board (page 78) or the Loaded Sweet Potato Fries Board (page 51).

Coconut Peanut Noodle Sauce

SOY-FREE, GLUTEN-FREE
Makes 1½ cups (360 ml)

1 teaspoon toasted sesame oil
2 cloves garlic, minced
1-inch (2.5 cm) piece ginger, peeled and grated
1 teaspoon red pepper flakes
½ cup (120 g) creamy salted peanut butter
1½ cups (360 ml) full-fat coconut milk
2 tablespoons (30 ml) lime juice
½ teaspoon salt

1 Heat the toasted sesame oil in a small saucepan over low heat. Add the garlic, ginger, and red pepper flakes and sauté for 1 minute.

2 Add the peanut butter and coconut milk to the saucepan and whisk to combine, scraping any stuck-on bits from the bottom of the saucepan.

3 Gently simmer the sauce for 5 minutes, until slightly thickened and ultra creamy. Remove from the heat and stir in the lime juice and salt.

4 Pour the sauce into a bowl and serve on the Coconut Peanut Noodle Bowls Board (page 71).

Mini Pie Crusts

Makes 12

Coconut oil cooking spray
2 vegan pie crusts (refrigerated and rolled up in a box)

1 Preheat the oven to 450°F (230°C or gas mark 8). Flip a standard-size muffin tin upside down (so the humps are sticking up) and mist with coconut oil cooking spray.

2 Lightly roll out the vegan pie crusts. Using a circular cookie cutter or a small prep bowl with a 4-inch (10 cm) diameter, create 12 mini pie crusts.

3 Working one at a time, lightly press each mini pie crust over the humps on the upside-down muffin tin.

4 Place the muffin tin on a baking sheet and bake the mini pie crusts for 10 minutes, until light golden in color. Remove the mini pie crusts from the oven and transfer them to a clean kitchen towel to cool.

5 Serve the mini pie crusts immediately on the Mini Berry Pie Board (page 112) or store them in an airtight container at room temperature for up to 2 days.

Quinoa Tabbouleh Salad

SOY-FREE, GLUTEN-FREE, NUT-FREE
Serves 4 to 6

½ cup (90 g) white quinoa
1 cup (240 ml) water
1 bunch curly parsley, finely chopped
¼ cup (15 g) fresh mint leaves, finely chopped
8 ounces (227 g) grape tomatoes, quartered
2 scallions (green part only), finely chopped
2 tablespoons (30 ml) olive oil
1 tablespoon (15 ml) lemon juice
1 clove garlic, minced
¼ teaspoon salt
Few twists of black pepper

1 Combine the quinoa and water in a small saucepan and bring to a boil over medium heat. Cover the saucepan and reduce the heat to low.

2 Simmer the quinoa for 10 minutes, or until the quinoa has completely absorbed the water. Remove from the heat and fluff the quinoa with a fork. Set aside to cool.

3 Add the parsley, mint, tomatoes, and scallions to a serving bowl.

4 To make the dressing, combine the olive oil, lemon juice, garlic, salt, and black pepper in a small jar. Secure the lid and shake vigorously to emulsify the ingredients. ➼

5 Once the quinoa has cooled, add it to the serving bowl and toss with the herbs and veggies. Drizzle the dressing over the salad and stir to combine.

6 Cover and refrigerate until ready to serve on the Mediterranean Grazing Board (page 39).

Roasted Beet Hummus

SOY-FREE, GLUTEN-FREE, NUT-FREE
Makes 1 cup (240 g)

1 large beet, roasted, peeled, and chopped
1 (15-ounce [420 g]) can chickpeas, drained and rinsed
3 tablespoons (45 ml) lemon juice
1 clove garlic, roughly chopped
2 tablespoons (30 g) tahini
¾ teaspoon salt
¼ cup (60 ml) olive oil, plus more for drizzling
1 teaspoon everything bagel seasoning, for topping (optional)

1 Place the beet, chickpeas, lemon juice, garlic, tahini, and salt in a food processor and turn it on. As the food processor runs, drizzle in the olive oil from the top.

2 Scoop the hummus into a bowl, cover, and refrigerate until ready to serve.

3 Just before serving, stir the hummus and add a swirl of olive oil to the top. Sprinkle with the everything bagel seasoning, if desired, and serve on the Ombré Farmers' Market Board (page 40) or the Build-Your-Own Bagel Sandwich Board (page 34).

Roasted Red Pepper Hummus

SOY-FREE, GLUTEN-FREE, NUT-FREE
Makes 1½ cups (360 g)

1 (15-ounce [420 g]) can chickpeas, drained and rinsed
½ cup (75 g) roasted red peppers, roughly chopped
2 tablespoons (30 g) tahini
2 tablespoons (30 ml) lemon juice
1 clove garlic, roughly chopped
½ teaspoon salt
1 tablespoon (15 ml) olive oil

1 Combine the chickpeas, roasted red peppers, tahini, lemon juice, garlic, and salt in the bowl of a food processor.

2 As you run the food processor, slowly drizzle the olive oil in through the top. Blend the hummus until completely smooth, about a minute. Taste and season with another pinch of salt if desired.

3 Scoop the hummus into a bowl, cover, and refrigerate until ready to serve on the Mediterranean Grazing Board (page 39).

Rustic Peach Jam with Thyme

SOY-FREE, GLUTEN-FREE, NUT-FREE
Makes 1 cup (240 g)

4 ripe yellow peaches
1 tablespoon (15 ml) lemon juice
3 tablespoons (45 ml) maple/agave syrup blend
1 large sprig fresh thyme
1 teaspoon tapioca starch

1 Peel the peaches and discard the skins. Slice the peaches into quarters and remove the pits.

2 Place the peach segments in a small saucepan and add the lemon juice, maple/agave syrup blend, and thyme. Turn the heat to low and use a silicone spatula to gently mash the peaches.

3 Simmer for 25 minutes, stirring occasionally, until the jam is fragrant and sticky.

4 Add the tapioca starch to a small bowl. Whisk in 1 tablespoon (15 ml) of the peach liquid until the tapioca starch has completely dissolved. Pour the mixture back into the saucepan and stir to combine.

5 Continue to simmer the jam for another 3 to 5 minutes, until it has thickened a bit more. Remove the thyme and discard.

6 Turn off the heat; the jam will continue to set as it cools to room temperature.

7 Scoop the jam into a bowl and serve on the Sweet and Savory Toast Board (page 23).

Smoky Roasted Carrots

NUT-FREE | *Serves 6*

4 medium carrots, peeled
1 teaspoon liquid smoke
1 tablespoon (15 ml) soy sauce
1 teaspoon avocado oil

1 Preheat the oven to 450°F (230°C or gas mark 8). Line a baking sheet with aluminum foil.

2 Use a vegetable peeler to slice the carrots into thin strips. Place the carrots in a bowl, add the liquid smoke, soy sauce, and avocado oil, and toss to coat.

3 Use tongs to transfer the carrots to the prepared baking sheet, leaving excess marinade in the bowl. Fold the aluminum foil into a packet so the carrots are completely enclosed.

4 Roast the carrots for 15 minutes. Return the carrots to the bowl and toss with the marinade once more. Transfer to a small bowl and serve on the Sweet and Savory Toast Board (page 23).

Strawberry Cashew Cheesecake Dip

GLUTEN-FREE, SOY-FREE | *Makes 2 cups (480 g)*

1½ cups (225 g) raw cashews, soaked
    overnight in water to cover
2 cups (300 g) fresh strawberries, halved
3 tablespoons (45 ml) lemon juice
¾ teaspoon vanilla extract
2 tablespoons (30 ml) maple syrup
¼ teaspoon salt

1 Drain the soaked cashews. Combine the cashews, strawberries, lemon juice, vanilla, maple syrup, and salt in the bowl of a food processor. Blend until creamy and smooth; adjust the sweetness to taste.

2 Enjoy immediately or store, covered, in the refrigerator until ready to serve on the Ombré Farmers' Market Board (page 40) or the Watermelon Pizza Board (page 118).

Blueberry Chia Pie Filling

SOY-FREE | *Makes 1 cup (240 g)*

12 ounces (336 g) blueberries,
    fresh or frozen
1½ tablespoons (18 g) coconut sugar
    or brown sugar
1½ teaspoons maple syrup
1 tablespoon (8 g) whole wheat flour
1 tablespoon (15 ml) water
1 tablespoon (8 g) chia seeds
¼ teaspoon lemon juice
Small pinch of salt

1 Combine the blueberries, coconut sugar, maple syrup, flour, and water in a small saucepan.

2 Bring to a gentle simmer over medium-low heat. Continue to simmer for 10 to 15 minutes, until the mixture has thickened slightly.

3 Remove from the heat and stir in the chia seeds, lemon juice, and salt. The filling will continue to thicken as it cools. ➥

4 Scoop the Blueberry Chia Pie Filling into a bowl and serve or cover and refrigerate until ready to enjoy on the Mini Berry Pie Board (page 112). If making ahead of time, warm on the stove just before serving.

Strawberry Chia Pie Filling

SOY-FREE | *Makes 1½ cups (360 g)*

1 pound (454 g) whole strawberries, fresh or frozen
1½ tablespoons (18 g) coconut sugar or brown sugar
1½ teaspoons maple syrup
1½ teaspoons whole wheat flour
1 tablespoon (15 ml) water
1 tablespoon (8 g) chia seeds
¼ teaspoon lemon juice
Small pinch of salt

1 Combine the strawberries, coconut sugar, maple syrup, flour, and water in a small saucepan.

2 Bring to a gentle simmer over medium-low heat. Continue to simmer for 15 to 20 minutes, until the mixture has thickened slightly. Use a spoon or spatula to smash some of the strawberries as they soften.

3 Remove from the heat and stir in the chia seeds, lemon juice, and salt. The filling will continue to thicken as it cools.

4 Scoop the Strawberry Chia Pie Filling into a bowl and serve on the Mini Berry Pie Board (page 112) or cover and refrigerate until ready to enjoy. If making ahead of time, warm on the stove just before serving.

Vegan Cheese Sauce

Makes 2½ cups (600 ml)

½ cup (70 g) raw cashews
1 cup (110 g) peeled and roughly chopped gold potato
½ cup (60 g) peeled and roughly chopped carrot
½ cup (80 g) roughly chopped yellow onion
1½ cups (360 ml) water
2 teaspoons miso paste
½ teaspoon Dijon mustard
1 tablespoon (15 ml) lemon juice
½ teaspoon paprika
2 tablespoons (12 g) nutritional yeast
1 tablespoon (8 g) tapioca starch
1 teaspoon salt

1 Combine the cashews, potato, carrot, and onion in a medium saucepan. Pour the water over the ingredients and bring to a boil over medium heat.

2 Cover, reduce the heat to low, and simmer for 12 minutes, until the veggies are very tender when pricked with a fork. Remove from the heat and leave the cover on the saucepan for another 5 minutes.

3 Pour the contents of the saucepan into a high-speed blender and add the miso paste, Dijon mustard, lemon juice, paprika, nutritional yeast, tapioca starch, and salt. Blend until completely creamy and smooth, about 1 minute. It might take a bit longer if you're using a standard blender.

4 Taste the vegan cheese sauce and adjust the ingredients if needed—I usually add a pinch more salt.

5 Use the sauce as directed in your recipe or pour into a container and allow the sauce to come to room temperature before covering and storing in the refrigerator.

Vegan Mac and Cheese

Serves 4

8 ounces (227 g) macaroni
1 cup (240 ml) Vegan Cheese Sauce (at left)
Salt and pepper, to taste

1 Bring a pot of water to a boil and pour in the macaroni. Cook until al dente, according to the package directions. Drain the pasta, but don't rinse.

2 Return the cooked macaroni to the pot. Pour in the Vegan Cheese Sauce and stir to coat. Season with salt and pepper, to taste.

Baked Tortilla Bowls

Makes 4

4 (10-inch [25 cm]) whole wheat tortillas
Coconut oil cooking spray

1 Preheat the oven to 375°F (190°C or gas mark 5). Take out a large baking sheet and cut four 12-inch (30 cm) squares of aluminum foil.

2 Place four oven-safe bowls or ramekins with a 4- to 5-inch (10 to 12.5 cm) diameter upside down on the baking sheet. Lightly mist both sides of a tortilla with coconut oil cooking spray and position the middle of the tortilla on the middle of one of the upside-down ramekins.

3 Place a piece of aluminum foil on top of the tortilla and use it to gently cover and fold the tortilla around the curved edges of the ramekin. Carefully turn the ramekin right-side up and tuck the ends of the aluminum foil inside. Repeat with the remaining tortillas.

4 With the ramekins right-side up, bake the tortilla bowls for 10 minutes.

5 Remove the baking sheet from the oven and use tongs to carefully remove the ramekins from the tortillas. Leave the foil in place, gently cradling the tortilla bowls. Bake for another 10 minutes, until the tortillas are crisp and hold their shape.

6 Serve the Baked Tortilla Bowls on the Taco Bowl Tuesday Board (page 72).

Banh Mi Pulled Jackfruit

NUT-FREE | *Serves 4*

1 (20-ounce [560 g]) can jackfruit in water or brine, drained and rinsed
¼ cup (60 ml) low-sodium soy sauce
2 tablespoons (30 ml) maple syrup
1 to 2 teaspoons chili garlic sauce
1 tablespoon (15 ml) lime juice
1 teaspoon toasted sesame oil
½ yellow onion, diced

1 Cut away the tough inner core from each piece of jackfruit (the part at the pointed end) and discard. Place the fleshy part of the jackfruit in a bowl and use clean hands or two forks to pull the pieces apart.

2 Rinse the jackfruit again, then squeeze out as much water as possible. Set aside.

3 Combine the soy sauce, maple syrup, chili garlic sauce, and lime juice in a small bowl.

4 Heat the toasted sesame oil in a large skillet over medium-low heat. Add the onion and sauté for 3 minutes.

5 Add the jackfruit to the skillet and increase the heat to medium. Drizzle in the sauce (it should sizzle) and toss to coat the jackfruit.

6 Continue to cook for another 5 minutes, stirring occasionally, until the jackfruit is deep golden and crispy on the edges. Remove from the heat and transfer to a bowl. Serve on the Vegan Banh Mi Board (page 46).

Basic Balsamic Vinaigrette

GLUTEN-FREE, SOY-FREE, NUT-FREE
Makes 1 cup (240 ml)

¼ cup (60 ml) balsamic vinegar
¾ cup (180 ml) olive oil
1 tablespoon (15 ml) maple syrup
¼ teaspoon salt
Several twists of black pepper

1 Combine the balsamic vinegar, olive oil, maple syrup, salt, and black pepper in a mason jar and secure the lid.

2 Shake the jar vigorously to emulsify the oil and vinegar. Taste the vinaigrette and adjust for sweetness and salt, if desired.

3 Store the dressing in the jar so it's easy to shake it up again when you're ready to serve.

Butternut Squash Soup Shooters

GLUTEN-FREE, SOY-FREE, NUT-FREE

Makes 8 (2-ounce [60 ml]) servings

12 ounces (336 g) butternut squash, cubed
(about 2 cups [336 g])
2 teaspoons olive oil, divided
½ teaspoon salt
½ teaspoon paprika
Several twists of black pepper
½ yellow onion, diced
2 cloves garlic, minced
1¼ cups (300 ml) vegetable broth

1 Preheat the oven to 400°F (200°C or gas mark 6) and line a baking sheet with parchment paper.

2 Spread the butternut squash cubes onto the prepared baking sheet and drizzle with 1 teaspoon of the olive oil. Sprinkle with the salt, paprika, and black pepper and toss to coat the squash in the oil and seasonings.

3 Roast the butternut squash until caramelized and fork tender, 20 to 25 minutes.

4 Warm the remaining 1 teaspoon olive oil in a medium saucepan over medium-low heat. When the oil is hot, add the onion and sauté for 3 minutes. Add the garlic to the saucepan and sauté for a minute more.

5 Pour in the vegetable broth and use a wooden spatula to loosen any stuck bits from the bottom of the pan. Add the roasted squash to the saucepan and simmer the ingredients for 5 minutes. Remove from the heat.

6 Carefully ladle the soup into a blender and blend until very smooth, 1 to 3 minutes, depending on your blender. Taste the soup (careful, it's hot!) and season with more salt if desired.

7 Pour the butternut squash soup into eight 2-ounce (60 ml) shot glasses and serve on the Fall Harvest Board (page 102).

Caramelized Onion Dip

Makes 1½ cups (360 g)

1 tablespoon (15 ml) olive oil
1 yellow onion, very thinly sliced
½ teaspoon salt
1 tablespoon (15 ml) water
2 (8-ounce [227 g]) packages plain vegan
cream cheese
¼ teaspoon garlic powder
¼ teaspoon onion powder
½ teaspoon vegan Worcestershire sauce
1 tablespoon (4 g) chopped fresh parsley,
plus more for topping

1 Warm the olive oil in a large skillet over medium-low heat. Add the onion and season with the salt.

2 Sauté the onion, stirring occasionally, for 15 minutes. The onion should be light golden brown and soft at this point.

3 Add the water to the skillet to rehydrate the onion and continue to cook, stirring occasionally, for another 10 minutes. When done, the onion should be deeply caramelized and very soft. Remove from the heat and transfer the onion to a cutting board.

4 When cool enough to handle, chop the caramelized onion and scrape it into a mixing bowl. Scoop the vegan cream cheese into the bowl and add the garlic powder, onion powder, vegan Worcestershire sauce, and fresh parsley. Stir to thoroughly combine the ingredients.

5 Scoop the caramelized onion dip into another bowl, cover, and refrigerate until ready to serve on the Winter Solstice Board (page 105).

Cauliflower Lentil Balls

GLUTEN-FREE, SOY-FREE, NUT-FREE | *Makes 28*

1¼ cups (100 g) gluten-free old-fashioned
    rolled oats
¼ cup ground (35 g) flaxseed
⅓ cup (80 ml) water
3 cups (300 g) cauliflower florets
1 (17.6-ounce [495 g]) package steamed
    lentils or 2½ cups (500 g) cooked lentils
½ teaspoon garlic powder
1 teaspoon onion powder
2 teaspoons dried oregano
1 teaspoon paprika
1 teaspoon salt
2 tablespoons (30 ml) olive oil, for cooking

1 Pour the oats into the bowl of a food processor and
run until the oats have broken down into a fine powder.
You should get 1 cup (100 g) oat flour. Transfer the
oat flour to a large mixing bowl and set aside.

In a small bowl, add the ground flaxseed and
water and stir to combine. Set aside to allow the
flax "egg" to set.

2 Bring a medium-size saucepan of water to a boil and
add the cauliflower florets. Boil the cauliflower until
just tender, about 5 minutes. Drain and transfer the
cauliflower to the bowl of your food processor.

3 Add the cooked lentils to the food processor and
pulse several times to chop up the cauliflower and
incorporate it with the lentils.

4 Scoop the cauliflower and lentil mixture into the
bowl with the oat flour. Add the garlic powder, onion
powder, oregano, paprika, salt, and flax mixture. Mix
thoroughly to combine all the ingredients; adjust the
seasonings to taste.

5 Heat the olive oil in a large, nonstick skillet over
medium-low heat. Roll the cauliflower and lentil
mixture between your hands to form balls the size of
golf balls. You should get 28 balls.

6 Place the cauliflower lentil balls in the hot skillet,
working in batches if needed. Use tongs to gently turn
the balls every 2 to 3 minutes, until they are golden
brown and crispy on all sides. Transfer the cauliflower
lentil balls to a plate lined with paper towels to cool.

7 Once cooled to room temperature, store the
cauliflower lentil balls in an airtight container in the
refrigerator or freezer until ready to serve on the
Teriyaki Cabbage Wraps Board (page 80) or the
Pizza Party Board (page 108).

Chickpea Salad Sandwiches

Makes 4

1 (15-ounce [420 g]) can chickpeas,
    drained and rinsed
3 tablespoons (45 g) vegan mayo, divided
1 tablespoon (15 g) creamy salted
    cashew butter
1 teaspoon Dijon mustard
1 cup (110 g) chopped celery
⅓ cup (45 g) dried cherries
1 tablespoon (8 g) capers
¼ teaspoon salt
1½ teaspoons finely chopped fresh dill
Several twists of black pepper
8 slices sandwich bread

1 Pour the chickpeas into a large mixing bowl and
add 1 tablespoon (15 g) of the vegan mayo. Use a
fork to smash the chickpeas against the bottom
and sides of the bowl until the mixture is about
90 percent mashed.

2 Add the remaining 2 tablespoons (30 g) vegan mayo,
cashew butter, Dijon mustard, celery, dried cherries,
capers, salt, and dill. Season with 8 to 10 twists of
black pepper and stir to combine all the ingredients. If
your chickpea salad looks a bit crumbly, continue to
mash the chickpeas until the mixture becomes sticky.

3 Scoop a ½ cup (120 g) portion of the chickpea salad
onto a piece of sandwich bread. Top with another
piece of bread and slice the sandwich in half. Repeat
with the remaining chickpea salad and bread slices.
Serve on the Front Yard Picnic Board (page 55).

Chickpea Scramble with Mushrooms

GLUTEN-FREE, SOY-FREE, NUT-FREE | *Serves 2*

1 teaspoon olive oil
1 shallot, finely chopped
1 clove garlic, minced
1 (15-ounce [420 g]) can chickpeas,
    drained and rinsed
½ teaspoon ground turmeric
¼ teaspoon salt
Several twists of black pepper
¼ cup (60 ml) vegetable broth
4 ounces (112 g) baby bella mushrooms,
    stems removed, sliced
1 tablespoon (1 g) snipped fresh chives

1 Warm the olive oil in a skillet over medium-low heat. When the oil is hot, add the shallot and garlic and sauté until soft and fragrant, 1 minute.

2 Add the drained chickpeas to the skillet and season with the turmeric, salt, and black pepper. Use a spoon or spatula to begin smashing some of the chickpeas against the bottom and sides of the skillet.

3 Pour the vegetable broth into the skillet and continue to stir and smash the chickpeas until the liquid cooks off and the chickpeas are quite soft, about 5 minutes.

4 Add the mushrooms and continue to sauté until the mushrooms are soft, another 4 to 5 minutes. Remove from the heat.

5 Taste the chickpea scramble and season with another pinch of salt if desired. Transfer to a plate and top with the fresh chives. Serve warm on the Breakfast in Bed Board (page 24) or the Vegan Breakfast Burrito Board (page 30).

Coconut Chickpea Curry

GLUTEN-FREE, SOY-FREE | *Serves 6*

1 tablespoon (15 g) coconut oil
1 large shallot, finely chopped
2 cloves garlic, minced
1½ teaspoons grated fresh ginger
3 tablespoons (45 g) curry paste
1 (15-ounce [420 g]) can tomato sauce
2 (15-ounce [420 g]) cans chickpeas,
    drained and rinsed
½ cup (120 ml) vegetable broth
1 (13.5-ounce [378 g]) can full-fat coconut milk

1 Warm the coconut oil in a large, deep skillet over medium-low heat. Add the shallot, garlic, and ginger and sauté for 3 minutes.

2 Add the curry paste to the skillet and sauté for another 3 minutes.

3 Pour the tomato sauce, chickpeas, and vegetable broth into the skillet and decrease the heat to low. Cover and simmer for 15 minutes.

4 Uncover the skillet and add the coconut milk. Continue to simmer until the curry has thickened slightly, about 15 minutes more.

5 Cover the Coconut Chickpea Curry to keep it warm until ready to serve on the Coconut Chickpea Curry Board (page 84).

Crispy Spiced Chickpeas

GLUTEN-FREE, SOY-FREE, NUT-FREE
Makes 1½ cups (300 g)

1 (15-ounce [420 g]) can chickpeas,
    drained and rinsed
2 teaspoons olive oil
½ teaspoon salt
1 teaspoon paprika (or spice of choice)

1 Preheat the oven to 400°F (200°C or gas mark 6) and line a rimmed baking sheet with parchment paper.

2 Spread the chickpeas onto a clean kitchen towel and place another towel on top. Use your hands to gently roll the chickpeas between the towels until

they are completely dry. Discard any loose chickpea skins that rub off.

3 Transfer the chickpeas to the prepared baking sheet. Drizzle with the olive oil and sprinkle with the salt. Shake the baking sheet to coat the chickpeas and place it in the oven. Roast the chickpeas for 25 minutes, shaking the pan halfway through.

4 Remove the chickpeas from the oven and sprinkle with the paprika while they're still hot. Shake the pan to coat the chickpeas in the paprika.

5 Let the Crispy Spiced Chickpeas cool slightly before serving on the Pantry Essentials Snack Board (page 43) or the Rainbow Chopped Salad Board (page 88). Store leftovers at room temperature and enjoy within 2 days for the best texture.

Edamame Mint Dip

GLUTEN-FREE, NUT-FREE
Makes 1½ cups (360 g)

1 (12-ounce [340 g]) bag frozen shelled edamame
1 (0.75-ounce [21 g]) package fresh mint leaves
½ cup (8 g) cilantro leaves
¼ cup (60 ml) lime juice
½ teaspoon salt
2 tablespoons (30 ml) water
2 tablespoons (30 ml) olive oil

1 Bring 4 cups (960 ml) water to a boil in a medium-size saucepan. Add the frozen edamame to the boiling water and cook for 4 minutes. Drain and rinse the edamame with cold water.

2 Transfer the edamame to the bowl of a food processor and add the mint, cilantro, lime juice, salt, and water.

3 Turn on the food processor and drizzle in the olive oil from the top as it runs. Blend until completely smooth.

4 Scoop the Edamame Mint Dip into a small bowl and serve on the Spring Forward Board (page 100) or store, covered, in the refrigerator until ready to serve.

Frosted Cranberries

GLUTEN-FREE, NUT-FREE, SOY-FREE
Makes 2 cups (300 g)

¼ cup (50 g) granulated sugar
¼ cup (60 ml) water
2 cups (300 g) fresh cranberries, sorted and rinsed
¼ cup (50 g) monk fruit or extra sugar

1 Combine the granulated sugar and water in a saucepan and bring to a simmer over low heat. Stir and simmer until the sugar dissolves. Remove from the heat.

2 Pour the cranberries into the saucepan and gently stir to coat the cranberries in the simple syrup.

3 Set a wire cooling rack over a rimmed baking sheet lined with parchment paper. Use a slotted spoon to transfer the cranberries from the saucepan to the wire rack. Allow the cranberries to drain and dry for 1 hour. When the cranberries are dry, discard the parchment paper.

4 Pour the monk fruit, or additional sugar if you aren't using monk fruit, onto the rimmed baking sheet. Transfer the sticky cranberries to the baking sheet and gently shake to roll the cranberries around in the monk fruit or sugar.

5 Transfer the frosted cranberries to an airtight container and store in the fridge until ready to serve on the New Year's Eve Champagne Toast Board (page 106).

Hearty Pinto and Black Bean Chili

GLUTEN-FREE, NUT-FREE, SOY-FREE
Serves 6

1 tablespoon (15 ml) olive oil
1 white onion, diced
3 cloves garlic, minced
2 tablespoons (16 g) chili powder
2 teaspoons ground cumin
1 teaspoon paprika
1 teaspoon salt
2 cups (480 ml) vegetable broth
2 tablespoons (30 g) tomato paste
1 (14.5-ounce [406 g]) can diced tomatoes
1 (15.5-ounce [434 g]) can pinto beans,
    drained and rinsed
1 (15.5-ounce [434 g]) can black beans,
    drained and rinsed
1½ cups (110 g) diced baby bella mushrooms

1 Warm the olive oil in a large stockpot over
   medium-low heat. Add the onion and garlic and
   sauté for 3 minutes.

2 Add the chili powder, cumin, paprika, and salt to the
   pot, stirring to coat the onion and garlic. Continue to
   cook for 2 minutes more.

3 Pour a splash of vegetable broth into the stockpot
   and use the tip of a wooden spatula to loosen any
   stuck bits from the bottom of the pot.

4 Add the remaining vegetable broth to the pot along
   with the tomato paste, diced tomatoes, pinto beans,
   black beans, and mushrooms.

5 Bring the chili to a gentle simmer over medium heat.
   Cover the pot, lower the heat slightly, and continue
   to cook for 20 minutes. Remove from the heat.

6 Serve immediately on the Loaded Vegan Chili Board
   (page 86). Leftover chili can be stored in an airtight
   container in the refrigerator for up to 5 days or in the
   freezer for up to 6 months.

Instant Pot Vegan Oatmeal

SOY-FREE, NUT-FREE | *Serves 4*

1 cup (80 g) steel-cut oats
2 cups (480 ml) water
1 cup (240 ml) oat milk
1 teaspoon vanilla extract
¼ teaspoon sea salt

1 Combine the steel-cut oats, water, oat milk, vanilla,
   and salt in an Instant Pot. Stir gently to combine.

2 Twist on the lid to lock and make sure the pressure
   valve is set to "sealing." Press "Pressure Cook" and
   make sure the "High Pressure" function is selected.
   Set the timer for 10 minutes.

3 When the Instant Pot beeps to indicate the oatmeal
   is done cooking, allow the pressure to release
   naturally for 15 to 20 minutes. Flip the pressure valve
   to release any remaining pressure. When the float
   valve drops, twist the lid to unlock and remove it.

4 The oatmeal will continue to thicken as it cools.
   If it thickens too much, stir in a splash of oat
   milk or water to loosen it up. Serve warm on the
   Grab-and-Go Oatmeal Board (page 26).

Lemon Artichoke Dip

GLUTEN-FREE, SOY-FREE, NUT-FREE
Makes 2 cups (480 g)

1 (12-ounce [340 g]) jar marinated
    artichoke hearts, drained
1 (15.5-ounce [434 g]) can Great Northern beans,
    drained and rinsed
3 tablespoons (45 ml) lemon juice
1 teaspoon dried oregano
¼ teaspoon salt
2 teaspoons olive oil, plus more for serving

1 Combine the artichoke hearts, beans, lemon juice,
   oregano, and salt in a food processor.

2 Run the food processor, drizzling in the olive oil,
   until the dip is creamy and smooth. Taste the dip and
   adjust the seasonings if needed. You should be able
   to taste the artichoke, lemon, and oregano.

3 Scoop the dip into a bowl, cover, and refrigerate until ready to serve. Swirl the dip with a touch more olive oil just before serving on the Netflix Night for Two Board (page 52).

Lemon Blueberry Quinoa Muffins

SOY-FREE | *Makes 12*

2 tablespoons (16 g) ground flaxseed
3 tablespoons (45 ml) water
1½ cups (290 g) cooked quinoa, cooled
2 cups (240 g) white whole wheat flour
½ cup (100 g) coconut sugar
1½ teaspoons baking powder
½ teaspoon salt
½ teaspoon lemon zest
1 cup (240 ml) oat milk
½ cup (120 g) coconut oil, melted
1 teaspoon vanilla extract
2 tablespoons (30 ml) maple syrup
3 tablespoons (45 ml) lemon juice
1½ cups (225 g) fresh blueberries

1 Preheat the oven to 425°F (220°C or gas mark 7) and put paper liners in the cups of a standard muffin tin.

2 In a small bowl, make a flax "egg" by combining the ground flaxseed with the water. Set aside to gel while you mix the batter.

3 In a large mixing bowl, add the quinoa, flour, coconut sugar, baking powder, salt, and lemon zest. Stir to combine.

4 In a smaller bowl, add the oat milk, melted coconut oil, vanilla, maple syrup, and lemon juice. Whisk to combine. If the coconut oil begins to solidify when it makes contact with the cold oat milk, microwave the ingredients for 30 seconds to 1 minute, until the coconut oil melts again and combines with the other liquid ingredients.

5 Begin pouring the wet ingredients into the dry ingredients while stirring. Add the flax "egg" to the bowl and stir to incorporate it into the batter. Finally, gently fold in the blueberries.

6 Divide the batter among the muffin cups, filling each to the top. If you have any leftover batter, add a square of parchment paper to a small baking sheet and spoon the batter onto it to make a bonus breakfast cookie.

7 Bake the muffins for 18 to 20 minutes, until a toothpick inserted into the center of a muffin comes out clean. If you're making breakfast cookies, bake for 10 to 12 minutes.

8 Allow the Lemon Blueberry Quinoa Muffins to cool in the pan for 5 minutes, then transfer the muffins to a wire rack to cool completely. Serve on the Post-Workout Lunch Board (page 63) or the Overnight Guest Welcome Board (page 64).

Note: *Store leftover muffins in an airtight container in the freezer for up to 3 months. Before serving, thaw frozen muffins completely at room temperature. Or reheat frozen muffins in the microwave for 30 seconds or in a 350°F (180°C or gas mark 4) oven for 10 to 15 minutes.*

Lemony Pea Pesto

GLUTEN-FREE, SOY-FREE
Makes 1 cup (240 g)

1 cup (150 g) fresh peas
1½ cups (90 g) packed basil leaves
1 tablespoon (4 g) nutritional yeast
¼ cup (35 g) raw almonds
½ teaspoon salt
1½ tablespoons (23 ml) lemon juice
1 large clove garlic
2 tablespoons (30 ml) water
⅓ cup (80 ml) olive oil

1 Combine the peas, basil, nutritional yeast, almonds, salt, lemon juice, garlic, and water in the bowl of a food processor and turn it on.

2 Drizzle in the olive oil from the top as the food processor runs. Pause to scrape down the sides of the bowl as needed. ➻

3 Taste the pesto and add a touch more lemon or salt, to taste.

4 Scoop the Lemony Pea Pesto into a bowl and serve on the Sunday Night Pasta Board (page 74).

Maple and Date Sweet Potato Dip

GLUTEN-FREE, SOY-FREE
Makes 1½ cups (360 g)

1½ pounds (680 g) sweet potatoes, peeled and diced into 1-inch (2.5 cm) cubes
¾ teaspoon ground cinnamon
1 teaspoon vanilla extract
¼ teaspoon ground nutmeg
½ teaspoon lemon juice
¾ teaspoon salt
2 tablespoons (30 ml) maple syrup, plus more for topping
4 dates, pitted
1 tablespoon (9 g) finely chopped candied pecans, for topping

1 Place the diced sweet potato in a large stockpot and cover with 1 inch (2.5 cm) of water. Bring to a boil over high heat, then lower the heat to medium and simmer for 15 to 20 minutes, until very tender. Drain the sweet potatoes and add them to the bowl of a food processor.

2 Add the cinnamon, vanilla, nutmeg, lemon juice, salt, and maple syrup to the food processor and blend until smooth, scraping down the sides of the bowl as needed.

3 Add the dates to the food processor and blend until the dates have broken down into small pieces; there should be some texture to the dip.

4 Scoop the Maple and Date Sweet Potato Dip into a bowl. Top with the candied pecans and another swirl of maple syrup just before serving on the Fall Harvest Board (page 102).

Mini Banana Bundt Cakes

SOY-FREE | *Makes 6*

Coconut oil cooking spray
2 cups (240 g) white whole wheat flour, plus more for dusting
1 cup (200 g) coconut sugar
1 teaspoon baking powder
½ teaspoon baking soda
½ teaspoon salt
2 ripe bananas, peeled
½ cup (120 g) coconut oil, melted
1 teaspoon vanilla extract
1 cup (240 ml) oat milk

1 Preheat the oven to 350°F (180°C or gas mark 4). Mist all six cavities of a mini Bundt pan (5-cup [1.2 L] capacity) with coconut oil cooking spray. Sprinkle a bit of flour into each cavity, making sure to cover all of the nooks and crannies.

2 In a large mixing bowl, whisk together the flour, sugar, baking powder, baking soda, and salt.

3 Place the bananas in a smaller bowl and mash with a fork. Add the melted coconut oil, vanilla, and oat milk and whisk, eliminating as many banana lumps as possible; a few lumps are okay.

4 Make a well in the middle of the dry ingredients. Begin pouring the wet ingredients into the dry ingredients while stirring. Mix the batter thoroughly, but don't overmix.

5 Divide the batter among the cavities in the mini Bundt pan, filling each one a little bit more than halfway (you may have a small amount of batter left over).

6 Bake for 20 minutes, until a toothpick inserted near the center comes out clean.

7 Cool the cakes in the pan for 10 minutes. Hold a wire cooling rack on top of the pan and flip it over to invert the cakes. Carefully lift the pan to release the cakes onto the cooling rack. Cool the Mini Banana Bundt Cakes for 15 minutes more before serving on the Mini Bundt Cakes Board (page 123).

Vanilla Glaze

GLUTEN-FREE, SOY-FREE
Makes ½ cup (120 ml)

1½ cups (180 g) confectioners' sugar
2½ tablespoons (37 ml) unsweetened almond milk
1 tablespoon (15 g) coconut oil
¼ teaspoon vanilla extract

1 Combine the confectioners' sugar, almond milk, coconut oil, and vanilla in a large mixing bowl.

2 Use an electric hand mixer to beat the ingredients together until smooth and drizzly, about 2 minutes.

3 Transfer the Vanilla Glaze to a small pitcher or creamer and serve with the Mini Banana Bundt Cakes on the Mini Bundt Cakes Board (page 123).

Miso Roasted Brussels Sprouts

NUT-FREE | *Serves 6*

1 pound (454 g) Brussels sprouts
2 teaspoons miso paste
1 tablespoon (15 ml) toasted sesame oil
1 large clove garlic, minced
¼ teaspoon salt, plus more for serving

1 Preheat the oven to 425°F (220°C or gas mark 7) and line a baking sheet with parchment paper.

2 Trim the woody ends off the Brussels sprouts and then cut them in half. Transfer the Brussels sprouts to a large mixing bowl.

3 In a smaller bowl, whisk together the miso paste, toasted sesame oil, garlic, and salt.

4 Drizzle the miso mixture over the Brussels sprouts and gently stir to coat the sprouts.

5 Spread the Brussels sprouts on the prepared baking sheet and arrange them cut-side down. Roast for 20 to 25 minutes, until tender and lightly caramelized. Season with a pinch more salt.

6 Serve the Miso Roasted Brussels Sprouts warm on the Winter Solstice Board (page 105).

Orange Vanilla Chia Pudding

GLUTEN-FREE, SOY-FREE | *Serves 1*

¾ cup (180 ml) unsweetened almond milk
¼ cup (35 g) chia seeds
½ teaspoon maple syrup
¼ teaspoon orange zest
⅛ teaspoon vanilla extract
Pinch of sea salt

1 Pour the almond milk into a glass. Sprinkle in the chia seeds and add the maple syrup, orange zest, vanilla, and sea salt. Whisk well to combine.

2 Refrigerate the chia pudding for at least 30 minutes. Serve on the Chia Pudding Parfait Board (page 20).

Pan con Tomate

SOY-FREE, NUT-FREE | *Serves 8*

4 ciabatta rolls, sliced in half
2 large cloves garlic, sliced in half
2 ripe beefsteak tomatoes, shredded on a box grater
Good olive oil
Flaky sea salt

1 Preheat the oven to 400°F (200°C or gas mark 6). Place the sliced ciabatta rolls cut-side down directly on the top rack of the oven and toast for 3 to 4 minutes. Remove from the oven and set aside to cool.

2 Rub the cut side of each piece of ciabatta bread with a clove of garlic.

3 Scoop the grated tomato into a small bowl.

4 Serve the toasted ciabatta on the Afternoon Tapas and Sangria Board (page 48) alongside the tomato, olive oil, and flaky sea salt. Allow each guest to top their own piece of ciabatta with tomato, a drizzle of olive oil, and a pinch or two of flaky sea salt.

Pimentón Roasted Carrots

GLUTEN-FREE, SOY-FREE, NUT-FREE
Serves 4

1 pound (454 g) petite carrots
1 tablespoon (15 ml) olive oil
1 tablespoon (15 ml) red wine vinegar
1 tablespoon (15 ml) maple syrup
1 teaspoon smoked paprika
½ teaspoon salt
Pinch of cayenne pepper

1 Preheat the oven to 400°F (200°C or gas mark 6) and line a baking sheet with parchment paper. Place the carrots in a single layer, evenly spaced, on the baking sheet.

2 Combine the olive oil, red wine vinegar, maple syrup, smoked paprika, salt, and cayenne pepper in a bowl and whisk.

3 Brush the carrots with the sauce, turning to coat the carrots on all sides. Leave excess marinade in the bowl.

4 Roast the carrots for 20 minutes, remove them from the oven, and brush with the spice sauce once again. Place the carrots back in the oven for another 30 minutes, until tender and caramelized.

5 Serve the carrots warm or at room temperature on the Afternoon Tapas and Sangria Board (page 48).

Pistachio Cabbage Slaw

GLUTEN-FREE, SOY-FREE | *Serves 6*

4 cups (280 g) shredded green cabbage
2 medium carrots, peeled and julienned
½ cup (8 g) cilantro, roughly chopped
2 teaspoons coconut oil
1 teaspoon whole cumin seed
½ teaspoon ground mustard seed
½ teaspoon ground ginger
Juice of ½ lime
¼ teaspoon sugar
Pinch of salt
¼ cup (35 g) roasted and salted pistachios

1 Combine the cabbage, carrots, and cilantro in a large bowl.

2 Warm the coconut oil in a small skillet over low heat. When the oil is hot, add the cumin seed, ground mustard seed, and ground ginger. Sauté the spices until fragrant, 1 minute.

3 Pour the coconut oil and spices over the vegetables. Add the lime juice, sugar, and salt and toss to coat. Add the pistachios to the bowl and refrigerate until ready to serve on the Coconut Chickpea Curry Board (page 84).

Pizza Dough Garlic Knots

NUT-FREE | *Makes 12*

1 pound (454 g) pizza dough
2 tablespoons (30 ml) olive oil or
    melted vegan butter
3 cloves garlic, minced
Pinch of salt
2 tablespoons (8 g) chopped fresh parsley

1 Preheat the oven to 425°F (220°C or gas mark 7) and line a large baking sheet with parchment paper.

2 Divide the pizza dough into 12 equal sections. This is easiest with a kitchen scale, but you can eyeball it if you don't have one.

3 Working one by one, roll the dough sections into 6-inch (15 cm)-long "snakes." Tie a knot with each piece of dough and space the knots evenly on the prepared baking sheet.

4 Combine the olive oil, garlic, and salt in a small bowl. Brush the tops and sides of each pizza dough knot with the garlic butter, reserving a bit for serving.

5 Bake the garlic knots for 12 to 15 minutes, until the tops are barely golden.

6 Remove the garlic knots from the oven. Stir the fresh parsley into the leftover garlic butter and brush the knots once again. Serve warm on the Pizza Party Board (page 108).

Pumpkin-Spiced Pumpkin Seeds

GLUTEN-FREE, SOY-FREE | *Makes 2 cups (280 g)*

2 cups (280 g) raw pumpkin seeds
2 teaspoons olive oil
1 tablespoon (8 g) ground cinnamon
½ teaspoon ground nutmeg
¼ teaspoon ground ginger
¼ teaspoon ground cloves
2 teaspoons coconut sugar
½ teaspoon salt
1 tablespoon (15 ml) maple syrup

1 Preheat the oven to 350°F (180°C or gas mark 4) and line a large rimmed baking sheet with parchment paper.

2 Pour the pumpkin seeds into a mixing bowl and drizzle with the olive oil. Toss to coat the pumpkin seeds in the oil.

3 In a small bowl, combine the cinnamon, nutmeg, ginger, cloves, coconut sugar, and salt.

4 Sprinkle the pumpkin spice mix over the pumpkin seeds, drizzle with the maple syrup, and toss to coat.

5 Spread the pumpkin seeds onto the prepared baking sheet and roast for 20 minutes, stirring the pumpkin seeds halfway through.

6 Allow the pumpkin seeds to cool on the baking sheet. When cool, transfer to a bowl and serve on the Thanksgiving Snack Board (page 96).

Quick Pickled Carrots or Red Onions

GLUTEN-FREE, SOY-FREE, NUT-FREE
Makes 2 cups (460 g)

2 tablespoons (25 g) sugar
¾ cup (180 ml) rice vinegar
½ cup (120 ml) hot water
¼ teaspoon salt
8 ounces (224 g) carrots, peeled and
   julienned, or red onions, thinly sliced
1-inch (2.5 cm) piece fresh ginger,
   peeled and thinly sliced

1 Combine the sugar, rice vinegar, hot water, and salt in a quart-sized jar and secure the lid. Shake vigorously until the sugar and salt dissolve.

2 Add the carrots or onions and sliced ginger to the jar and gently press down with a spoon to submerge the carrots or onions and ginger in the pickling liquid. Secure the lid and allow the mixture to come to room temperature before transferring the jar to the fridge.

3 The flavor of these quick pickled vegetables will improve the longer they sit, so try to make them a day or two before serving the carrots on the Vegan Banh Mi Board (page 46) or the red onions on the Mediterranean Grazing Board (page 39).

Red Sangria

GLUTEN-FREE, SOY-FREE, NUT-FREE
Serves 8

2 (750 ml) bottles Rioja wine, Tempranillo,
   or Garnacha (sometimes labeled Grenache)
   or a blend
½ cup (120 ml) triple sec
¼ cup (60 ml) maple syrup
2 oranges (1½ oranges juiced and
   ½ orange sliced and quartered)
1 Granny Smith apple, cored and sliced
1½ cups (225 g) strawberries, quartered
Ice, for serving
1 (750 ml) bottle cava, chilled

1 Combine the wine, triple sec, maple syrup, orange juice, orange slices, apple slices, and strawberries in a large pitcher and stir to combine. Taste and add more sweetener if desired.

2 Refrigerate the sangria for at least 6 hours, overnight preferred. Serve with ice and cava on the Afternoon Tapas and Sangria Board (page 48). Leftover sangria will keep in the fridge for up to 2 days.

Red Wine Vinaigrette

GLUTEN-FREE, SOY-FREE, NUT-FREE
Makes 1 cup (240 ml)

¼ cup (60 ml) red wine vinegar
¾ cup (180 ml) olive oil
1 teaspoon Dijon mustard
¼ teaspoon salt
Several twists of black pepper

1 Combine the red wine vinegar, olive oil, Dijon mustard, salt, and black pepper in a glass mason jar and secure the lid.

2 Shake the jar vigorously to emulsify the oil and vinegar.

3 Store the dressing in the jar so it's easy to shake it up again. Serve on the Stone Fruit Panzanella Salad Board (page 45).

Roasted Tomato Soup with Rosemary

GLUTEN-FREE, SOY-FREE | *Serves 4*

2½ pounds (1135 g) ripe beefsteak tomatoes
½ yellow onion, sliced into thick wedges
1½ cups (150 g) cauliflower florets
2 tablespoons (30 ml) olive oil, divided
1 teaspoon salt, divided
Several twists of black pepper
1 head garlic, unpeeled
3 cups (720 ml) vegetable broth
1 tablespoon (2 g) chopped fresh rosemary
¼ cup (35 g) raw cashews
2 teaspoons maple syrup

1 Preheat the oven to 400°F (200°C or gas mark 6) and line two rimmed baking sheets with parchment paper.

2 Core and quarter the tomatoes and place them on the baking sheets along with the onion and cauliflower. Drizzle the veggies with 1½ tablespoons (23 ml) of the olive oil and season with ½ teaspoon of the salt and several twists of black pepper. Toss to coat.

3 Place the head of garlic on a small square of aluminum foil and drizzle with the remaining ½ tablespoon (7 ml) olive oil. Fold up the edges and twist the top to secure the garlic in the foil packet. Place it on one of the baking sheets.

4 Put both baking sheets on the middle rack of your oven and roast for 35 minutes, until the vegetables are very tender and slightly caramelized.

5 Scoop the roasted tomatoes, onion, and cauliflower into a large stockpot. When the garlic is cool enough to handle, squeeze each clove out of its skin and add to the pot. Pour in the vegetable broth and add the remaining ½ teaspoon salt. Stir in the rosemary, cashews, and maple syrup.

6 Bring the soup to a gentle simmer over medium heat. Decrease the heat to low and continue to simmer for 30 minutes to allow the flavors to meld. Turn off the heat and allow the soup to cool slightly.

7 Carefully ladle the soup into a blender, working in batches if necessary, and blend until creamy and very smooth. Pour the blended tomato soup back into the pot and return to low heat until ready to serve on the Grilled Cheese and Roasted Tomato Soup Board (page 83).

Rosemary Mashed Potatoes

GLUTEN-FREE, SOY-FREE | *Serves 4 to 6*

2 pounds (908 g) Yukon gold potatoes, peeled and quartered
1 tablespoon (15 ml) olive oil
3 large cloves garlic, minced
1 tablespoon (2 g) finely chopped fresh rosemary
½ cup (120 ml) plain unsweetened almond milk
1½ teaspoons salt
A few twists of black pepper

1 Add the potatoes to a large stockpot and cover with 1 inch (2.5 cm) of water. Bring to a boil over high heat, then decrease the heat to medium-low and simmer until the potatoes are very tender, 20 to 25 minutes. Drain and rinse the potatoes and return them to the pot.

2 Add the olive oil to a small skillet and warm over low heat. When the oil is hot, add the garlic and sauté until light golden, about 1 minute.

3 Pour the contents of the skillet into the stockpot with the potatoes. Add the rosemary, almond milk, salt, and pepper to the potatoes and mash with a potato masher. Season with salt to taste.

4 Scoop the Rosemary Mashed Potatoes into a bowl and serve on the Thanksgiving Snack Board (page 96).

Salted Hot Chocolate

GLUTEN-FREE, SOY-FREE | *Serves 4*

4 cups (960 ml) unsweetened plain almond milk
¾ cup (130 g) semisweet vegan chocolate chips
½ teaspoon flaky sea salt

1 Pour the almond milk into a saucepan and place over medium heat. Once you start to see bubbles form around the edges of the pan, add the vegan chocolate chips and flaky sea salt.

2 Whisk the ingredients together until the chocolate has completely melted. Decrease the heat to low and gently simmer for 5 minutes, until the hot chocolate is velvety smooth.

3 Pour into a thermal or insulated carafe and serve warm on the Hot Chocolate Dessert Board (page 126).

Sautéed Mushrooms

GLUTEN-FREE, SOY-FREE, NUT-FREE
Serves 4

1 teaspoon olive oil
8 ounces (227 g) baby bella mushrooms, halved
¼ teaspoon salt
Several twists of black pepper
½ teaspoon dried thyme

1 Warm the olive oil in a nonstick skillet over medium heat. When the oil is hot, add the mushrooms and season with the salt, black pepper, and thyme.

2 Sauté the mushrooms until golden and tender, about 4 minutes.

3 Scoop the Sautéed Mushrooms into a bowl and serve on the Sunday Night Pasta Board (page 74) or the Pizza Party Board (page 108).

Savory Dill Popcorn

GLUTEN-FREE, SOY-FREE
Makes 10 cups (500 g)

4 tablespoons (60 ml) melted coconut oil, divided
½ cup (100 g) popcorn kernels
2 tablespoons (8 g) nutritional yeast
1 tablespoon (4 g) finely chopped fresh dill
¼ teaspoon garlic powder
½ teaspoon salt

1 Pour 1 tablespoon (15 ml) of the melted coconut oil into a large stockpot with a tight-fitting lid. Add 3 popcorn kernels, put the lid on the pot, and place over low heat.

2 Once all 3 popcorn kernels have popped, pour the remaining popcorn kernels into the pot and replace the lid. Pop the popcorn for about 3 minutes, shaking the pot frequently to prevent the kernels from burning.

3 When the popping slows down, turn off the heat and uncover the popcorn. Drizzle with the remaining 3 tablespoons (45 ml) coconut oil. Place the lid back on the pot and shake to coat the popcorn in the oil.

4 In a small bowl, combine the nutritional yeast, fresh dill, garlic powder, and salt. Sprinkle a third of the seasoning over the popcorn, cover the pot with the lid, and shake to coat. Repeat until you've used all of the seasoning and the popcorn is lightly coated with the herbs and spices.

5 Transfer the Savory Dill Popcorn to a large bowl and serve on the Family Movie Night Board (page 56).

Spiced Potatoes and Cauliflower

GLUTEN-FREE, SOY-FREE, NUT-FREE
Serves 6

1¼ pounds (668 g) Yukon gold potatoes,
    cut into 1-inch (2.5 cm) pieces
4 cups (400 g) cauliflower florets
3 tablespoons (45 ml) olive oil
½ teaspoon ground turmeric
1 teaspoon ground cumin
½ teaspoon ground coriander
1½ teaspoons garam masala
¼ teaspoon garlic powder
½ teaspoon salt
½ cup (75 g) peas, fresh or frozen
    and thawed

1 Preheat the oven to 400°F (200°C or gas mark 6).

2 Spread the potatoes and cauliflower on a large rimmed baking sheet and drizzle with the olive oil.

3 In a small bowl, mix together the turmeric, cumin, coriander, garam masala, garlic powder, and salt. Sprinkle the spices over the veggies and toss to coat.

4 Roast the potatoes and cauliflower for 40 minutes, stirring halfway through.

5 Remove the baking sheet from the oven and add the peas. Return the baking sheet to the oven for another 5 minutes, until all of the vegetables are fork tender. Turn the oven temperature down to 200°F (100°C or gas mark ½).

6 Keep the Spiced Potatoes and Cauliflower warm in the oven until ready to serve on the Coconut Chickpea Curry Board (page 84).

Sweet Potato Brownie Bowls

SOY-FREE | *Makes 2*

1 medium sweet potato, peeled and diced
    into ½-inch (1.3 cm) cubes (2 cups [280 g])
1 tablespoon (8 g) ground flaxseed
1½ tablespoons (23 ml) water
¼ cup (30 g) unsweetened cocoa powder
½ cup (60 g) white whole wheat flour
½ teaspoon baking powder
1 teaspoon vanilla extract
1 teaspoon salt
¼ cup (50 g) coconut sugar
1 tablespoon (15 ml) coconut oil
2 tablespoons (30 ml) oat milk
¼ cup (45 g) vegan semisweet chocolate chips,
    plus more for topping
Coconut oil cooking spray

1 Preheat the oven to 325°F (170°C or gas mark 3) and bring a saucepan of water to a rapid boil. Add the diced sweet potato to the water and boil until very tender, 15 minutes. Drain the sweet potato chunks and transfer them to the bowl of a food processor fitted with the chopping/mixing blade (also known as the "S" blade).

2 To make a flax "egg," combine the ground flaxseed and water in a small bowl. Set it aside to gel.

3 Add the cocoa powder, flour, baking powder, vanilla, salt, coconut sugar, coconut oil, and oat milk to the food processor. Blend, stopping to scrape down the sides of the bowl as needed, until very smooth. Add the flax "egg" and process for another 10 seconds. Carefully remove the blade from the bowl of your food processor and stir in the vegan chocolate chips.

4 Mist the inside of two 5-ounce (140 g) oven-safe ramekins with coconut oil cooking spray. Divide the batter between the ramekins and smooth out the tops. Sprinkle a few more chocolate chips on the top of each brownie bowl.

5 Bake the brownie bowls until a toothpick inserted into the center comes out clean, 30 minutes. Transfer the bowls to a wire rack and allow them to cool for at least 20 minutes before serving on the Netflix Night for Two Board (page 52).

Tempeh Sloppy Joes

Serves 4

1 (8-ounce [227 g]) package tempeh
1 cup (160 g) diced yellow onion
4 cloves garlic, roughly chopped
1 teaspoon olive oil
1 tablespoon (15 g) tomato paste
1 (15-ounce [420 g]) can tomato sauce
2 tablespoons (30 ml) maple syrup
½ teaspoon Dijon mustard
1 teaspoon apple cider vinegar
1 teaspoon vegan Worcestershire sauce
1 tablespoon (15 ml) soy sauce
1 tablespoon (8 g) chili powder
½ teaspoon paprika
½ teaspoon salt, plus more to taste

1 Fill a deep skillet with ½ inch (1.3 cm) of water and slice the tempeh into 1-inch (2.5 cm) pieces. Place the tempeh pieces in the skillet and bring to a simmer over medium heat. Cover, decrease the heat to low, and continue to simmer the tempeh for 10 minutes. Remove the tempeh from the skillet with a slotted spoon and transfer to the bowl of a food processor.

2 Add the onion and garlic to the food processor and pulse a few times to break up the tempeh, onion, and garlic into small, crumbly pieces.

3 Drain the water from the skillet and wipe dry. Add the olive oil and warm over medium heat. Add the tempeh mixture to the skillet and sauté for 5 minutes, until the tempeh has browned slightly and the onion and garlic are fragrant.

4 Add the tomato paste, tomato sauce, maple syrup, Dijon mustard, apple cider vinegar, vegan Worcestershire sauce, soy sauce, chili powder, paprika, and salt to the skillet and stir to combine. Cover, decrease the heat to low, and simmer for 15 minutes. Taste and add a pinch more salt, if desired.

5 Transfer the Tempeh Sloppy Joes filling to a bowl and serve on the Build-Your-Own Sloppy Joes Board (page 77). Store leftover Sloppy Joe filling, covered, in the refrigerator for up to 3 days.

Vegan Beer Cheese Dip

Makes 1¾ cups (420 ml)

1 teaspoon olive oil
2 cloves garlic, minced
1½ cups (360 ml) Vegan Cheese Sauce (page 134)
½ cup (60 ml) beer (pilsner or lager),
    plus more to taste
½ teaspoon salt

1 Warm the olive oil in a small saucepan over low heat. Add the garlic and sauté until fragrant and light golden in color, 30 seconds.

2 Pour in the Vegan Cheese Sauce and beer. Turn up the heat slightly to maintain a very gentle simmer; you should see bubbles around the edges of the saucepan.

3 Continue to simmer for 10 minutes, until the dip has thickened slightly. Season with the salt and remove from the heat.

4 Pour the Vegan Beer Cheese Dip into a bowl and serve on the Oktoberfest Grazing Board (page 99) or cool to room temperature and refrigerate until ready to serve.

Vegan Chocolate Sauce

GLUTEN-FREE, SOY-FREE | *Makes 1 cup (240 g)*

1 (10-ounce [280 g]) bag vegan semisweet
    chocolate chunks (1½ cups [280 g])
⅓ cup (80 ml) coconut milk, plus more
    as needed
Pinch of salt

1 Pour the chocolate chunks into a glass bowl. Microwave in 30-second intervals, stirring in between, until the chocolate is halfway melted. Alternatively, you can melt the chocolate on the stove using a double boiler.

2 When the chocolate is halfway melted, pour the coconut milk into the bowl. Continue to microwave or warm the chocolate in the double boiler until all of the chunks have melted and the sauce is smooth and drizzly. If the chocolate is too thick, add more ➤➤

coconut milk, 1 tablespoon (15 ml) at a time, until it reaches the proper consistency. Stir in a pinch of salt.

3   Pour the Vegan Chocolate Sauce into a bowl and serve on the Chocolate Fondue Board (page 116), the Mini Bundt Cakes Board (page 123), or the Ice Cream Sundae Board (page 124).

Vegan Grilled Cheese Sandwich

Makes 1 sandwich

2 slices sourdough sandwich bread
2 teaspoons vegan butter or olive oil
3 tablespoons (45 ml) Vegan Cheese Sauce (page 134)

1   Preheat a cast-iron skillet over medium heat. Spread the vegan butter on one side of each slice of bread.

2   Spread the cheese sauce over the non-buttered side of one of the slices of bread and place the other piece of bread on top, buttered-side out.

3   Carefully place the grilled cheese in the hot skillet and cook until toasted and golden brown, about 2 to 3 minutes on each side.

4   Transfer the Vegan Grilled Cheese Sandwich to a cutting board, slice in half, and serve on the Grilled Cheese and Roasted Tomato Soup Board (page 83).

Veggie Taco Crumbles

Serves 4

12 ounces (336 g) baby bella mushrooms, roughly chopped
2 cups (200 g) cauliflower florets
⅓ cup (45 g) raw walnuts
¼ cup (30 g) sun-dried tomatoes, drained
1 teaspoon olive oil
¼ cup (40 g) finely diced red onion
3 cloves garlic, minced
2 tablespoons (16 g) chili powder
1 tablespoon (15 ml) soy sauce
1 tablespoon (15 ml) salsa
2 teaspoons ground cumin
1 teaspoon paprika
½ teaspoon salt, plus more to taste

1   Preheat the oven to 375°F (190°C or gas mark 5) and line a large baking sheet with parchment paper.

2   Place the mushrooms, cauliflower, walnuts, and sun-dried tomatoes in the bowl of a food processor. Pulse a few times, scraping down the sides of the bowl as needed, until the ingredients are finely chopped.

3   Warm the olive oil in a large skillet over medium-low heat. When hot, add the onion and garlic and sauté for 3 minutes.

4   Add the mushroom mixture to the skillet along with the chili powder, soy sauce, salsa, cumin, paprika, and salt. Sauté for another 8 to 10 minutes, until the veggies have reduced in volume by more than half. Remove from the heat and season with more salt, to taste.

5   Spread the taco crumble mixture on the prepared baking sheet in an even layer and bake for 15 minutes, stirring at the halfway point. When done, the crumbles should be browned and slightly crumbly.

6   Remove the taco crumbles from the oven and cool directly on the baking sheet. Serve on the Taco Bowl Tuesday Board (page 72).

Warm Arugula and Artichoke Dip

Makes 2 cups (480 ml)

1 (7-ounce [196 g]) bag fresh arugula
¼ cup (60 ml) water
1 (14-ounce [392 g]) can whole artichoke hearts
2 cloves garlic, finely chopped
2 (8-ounce [227 g]) packages plain vegan cream cheese
¼ cup (60 g) hummus
2 tablespoons (30 ml) lemon juice
½ teaspoon salt
Several twists of black pepper

1 Preheat the oven to 350°F (180°C or gas mark 4).

2 Empty the bag of arugula into a large, deep-sided skillet and add the water. Cover the skillet and steam the arugula over low heat for 3 minutes, until wilted.

3 Transfer the steamed arugula to a clean kitchen towel. When cool enough to handle, squeeze the moisture from the arugula until very dry. Roughly chop the arugula and place it in a mixing bowl.

4 Drain the can of artichoke hearts. Using clean hands, squeeze the artichoke hearts to remove as much liquid as possible. Transfer the artichoke hearts to a cutting board and roughly chop. Add the chopped artichokes to the mixing bowl with the arugula.

5 Add the chopped garlic, vegan cream cheese, hummus, lemon juice, salt, and black pepper to the mixing bowl and stir to thoroughly combine the ingredients.

6 Spoon the mixture into a small oven-safe dish and bake for 25 minutes, until the dip is heated through and slightly golden on top. Serve warm with crackers, veggies, and baguette on the Spring Forward Board (page 100).

Whipped Sweet Potato and Carrots

Serves 4

2 medium sweet potatoes, scrubbed clean
8 ounces (227 g) carrots, peeled and cut into ½-inch (1.3 cm) chunks
1½ teaspoons olive oil
¼ teaspoon salt, plus more to taste
¼ cup (60 ml) oat milk
1 tablespoon (14 g) vegan butter

1 Preheat the oven to 400°F (200°C or gas mark 6) and line two baking sheets with parchment paper.

2 Prick the sweet potatoes with a fork and place them on one of the baking sheets. Roast the sweet potatoes for 50 to 60 minutes, until very tender when pierced with a fork.

3 Place the carrot chunks in a mixing bowl, drizzle with the olive oil, and sprinkle with the salt. Toss to coat. Arrange the pieces in a single layer on the other baking sheet. Once the sweet potatoes have been roasting for 20 minutes, add the carrots to the oven. Roast the carrots for 30 to 40 minutes, until very tender.

4 Slice the sweet potatoes in half lengthwise and set them aside to cool.

5 When cool enough to handle, scoop the sweet potato flesh into a large mixing bowl. Add the roasted carrots, oat milk, and vegan butter.

6 Use an electric hand mixer to whip the sweet potatoes and carrots until smooth and fluffy, about 2 minutes. Season with salt to taste.

7 Scoop the Whipped Sweet Potato and Carrots into a bowl and serve on the Sweet Potato Breakfast Bowls Board (page 32).

Acknowledgments

WRITING AND PHOTOGRAPHING A COOKBOOK during a pandemic was more challenging than I ever could have imagined. I am so grateful to have had the love and support of many wonderful people along the way who made *Vegan Boards* possible. I have to start by thanking my husband, Andrew. From tackling the dirty dishes so I could edit photos to making sure I was fed every night, he was essential to this cookbook getting done. Thank you, Ange.

A very special thanks to Katie Koteen, who in 2014 took a chance on hiring a freelance writer she had never met to help manage her blog, *Well Vegan*. You saw my potential and passion and your openness and generosity changed my life. I never thought I'd get the opportunity to write one cookbook, let alone two. I couldn't ask for a more supportive creative partner and colleague.

Thanks to everyone at The Harvard Common Press for making this cookbook possible. A special thank you to my editor, Dan Rosenberg, for your insight and for being patient with my never-ending string of questions during the production of this cookbook. Thanks to the talented Heather Godin for bringing the cover and design of *Vegan Boards* to life.

I'd also like to thank my parents, Dave and Carole Kasbee, who lovingly insisted on family dinners throughout my childhood. Our evenings at the dinner table are some of my fondest memories of being a kid. I owe my love of food and cooking to you, Dad. Additionally, thank you to my new family, Tony and Carol Pelletier and Katie, Chris, and Benjamin Ragona, for your constant love and support.

Thank you, Marie Reginato, for being so kind and offering me advice on cookbook photography. When I had no idea where to start, you gave me the confidence boost I needed.

I can't acknowledge all of the wonderful beings in my life without mentioning my very special dog, Rex. His constant supervision of the cooking, writing, and photographing of *Vegan Boards* was equal parts annoying and adorable. I am so grateful for his companionship.

Finally, I'd like to thank the readers and followers of *Well Vegan*. Your enthusiasm for plant-based cooking and eating allows me to continue creating recipes and doing work that I absolutely love. Thank you.

About the Author

KATE KASBEE CREATES, COOKS, WRITES, and photographs recipes for the popular vegan blog *Well Vegan* (wellvegan.com). She and her partner on the blog, Katie Koteen, are the coauthors of *Frugal Vegan: Affordable, Easy, and Delicious Vegan Cooking.* Kate's recipes and writing have been featured on Refinery29, Huffington Post, MindBodyGreen, OneGreenPlanet, BuzzFeed, and Oprah.com, among other destinations. A native of the Midwest and a certified plant-based chef, Kate lives in Los Angeles.

Index

A

Adobo Sauce, Sweet and Spicy, 130
Afternoon Tapas and Sangria Board, 48–49
artichokes
    Lemon Artichoke Dip, 140–41
    Warm Arugula and Artichoke Dip, 150–51
Arugula and Artichoke Dip, Warm, 150–51

B

Backyard Campfire Board, 60–61
Bagel Sandwich Board, Build-Your-Own, 34–35
Baked Tortilla Bowls, 135
Balsamic Vinaigrette, Basic, 135
bananas
    Frozen Banana Pops Board, 114–15
    Mini Banana Bundt Cakes, 110, 142
Banh Mi Board, Vegan, 46–47
Banh Mi Pulled Jackfruit, 135
Basic Balsamic Vinaigrette, 135
BBQ Tempeh Burgers, 128
beans
    Chickpea Salad Sandwiches, 137
    Chickpea Scramble with Mushrooms, 138
    Coconut Chickpea Curry, 138
    Crispy Spiced Chickpeas, 138–39
    Hearty Pinto and Black Bean Chili, 68, 140
    Loaded Vegan Chili Board, 68, 86–87
Beer Cheese Dip, Vegan, 149

Beet Hummus, Roasted, 132
Berry Pie Board, Mini, 112–13
blueberries
    Blueberry Chia Pie Filling, 133–34
    Lemon Blueberry Quinoa Muffins, 141
breakfast and brunch boards
    Breakfast in Bed Board, 24–25
    Build-Your-Own Bagel Sandwich Board, 34–35
    Chia Pudding Parfait Board, 20–21
    Grab-and-Go Oatmeal Board, 26–27
    Sweet and Savory Toast Board, 22–23
    Sweet and Spicy Melon Sparkler Board, 18, 28–29
    Sweet Potato Breakfast Bowls Board, 32–33
    Vegan Breakfast Burrito Board, 30–31
Breakfast in Bed Board, 24–25
Brownie Bowls, Sweet Potato, 36, 148
Brussels Sprouts, Miso Roasted, 143
Buffalo Sauce, Classic, 129
Build-Your-Own Bagel Sandwich Board, 34–35
Build-Your-Own Sloppy Joes Board, 76–77
Bundt cakes
    Mini Banana Bundt Cakes, 110, 142
    Mini Bundt Cakes Board, 110, 122–23
Burgers, BBQ Tempeh, 128
Burrito Board, Vegan Breakfast, 30–31
Butternut Squash Soup Shooters, 136

C

cabbage
 Pistachio Cabbage Slaw, 144
 Teriyaki Cabbage Wraps Board, 80–81
Caramelized Onion Dip, 136
carrots
 Carrot Dogs, 128
 Pimentón Roasted Carrots, 144
 Quick Pickled Carrots or Red Onions, 145
 Smoky Roasted Carrots, 133
 Whipped Sweet Potato and Carrots, 151
cashews
 Strawberry Cashew Cheesecake Dip, 133
 Vegan Beer Cheese Dip, 149
 Vegan Cheese Sauce, 134
 Vegan Grilled Cheese Sandwich, 150
cauliflower
 Cauliflower Lentil Balls, 137
 Cauliflower Wings, 129
 Game Day Cauliflower Wings Board, 92–93
 Spiced Potatoes and Cauliflower, 148
 Veggie Taco Crumbles, 150
Champagne Toast Board, New Year's Eve, 90,
 106–7
Cheese Board, Date Night Vegan, 58–59
Cheese Dip, Vegan Beer, 149
Cheese Sandwich, Vegan Grilled, 150
Cheese Sauce, Vegan, 134
Chia Pudding Parfait Board, 20–21
chia seeds
 Blueberry Chia Pie Filling, 133–34
 Orange Vanilla Chia Pudding, 143
 Strawberry Chia Pie Filling, 134
chickpeas
 Chickpea Salad Sandwiches, 137
 Chickpea Scramble with Mushrooms, 138
 Coconut Chickpea Curry, 138
 Crispy Spiced Chickpeas, 138–39

chili
 Cincinnati-Style Chili Dinner Board, 78–79
 Cincinnati-Style Vegan Chili, 130–31
 Hearty Pinto and Black Bean Chili, 68, 140
 Loaded Vegan Chili Board, 68, 86–87
chocolate
 Chocolate-Dipped Pretzel Sparklers, 130
 Chocolate Fondue Board, 116–17
 Hot Chocolate Dessert Board, 126–27
 Salted Hot Chocolate, 147
 Sweet Potato Brownie Bowls, 36, 148
 Vegan Chocolate Sauce, 149–50
Cincinnati-Style Chili Dinner Board, 78–79
Cincinnati-Style Vegan Chili, 130–31
Classic Buffalo Sauce, 129
Coconut Chickpea Curry, 138
Coconut Chickpea Curry Board, 84–85
Coconut Peanut Noodle Bowls Board, 70–71
Coconut Peanut Noodle Sauce, 131
Cranberries, Frosted, 139
Crispy Spiced Chickpeas, 138–39
Curry, Coconut Chickpea, 138

D

Date Night Vegan Cheese Board, 58–59
Date Sweet Potato Dip, Maple and, 142
dips
 Caramelized Onion Dip, 136
 Edamame Mint Dip, 139
 Lemon Artichoke Dip, 140–41
 Maple and Date Sweet Potato Dip, 142
 Strawberry Cashew Cheesecake Dip, 133
 Vegan Beer Cheese Dip, 149
 Warm Arugula and Artichoke Dip, 150–51

E

Edamame Mint Dip, 139

F

Fall Harvest Board, 102–3
Family Movie Night Board, 56–57
Friday Happy Hour Board, 66–67
Front Yard Picnic Board, 54–55
Frosted Cranberries, 139
Frozen Banana Pops Board, 114–15
fruit and dessert boards
    Chocolate Fondue Board, 116–17
    Frozen Banana Pops Board, 114–15
    Hot Chocolate Dessert Board, 126–27
    Ice Cream Sundae Board, 124–25
    Mini Berry Pie Board, 112–13
    Mini Bundt Cakes Board, 110, 122–23
    Watermelon Pizza Board, 118–19
    Winter Yogurt Waffle Bowls Board, 120–21

G

Game Day Cauliflower Wings Board, 92–93
garlic
Pizza Dough Garlic Knots, 144
    Sticky Sesame Garlic Sauce, 129
    Grab-and-Go Oatmeal Board, 26–27
grazing at home boards, 13
    Afternoon Tapas and Sangria Board, 48–49
    Backyard Campfire Board, 60–61
    Date Night Vegan Cheese Board, 58–59
    Family Movie Night Board, 56–57
    Friday Happy Hour Board, 66–67
    Front Yard Picnic Board, 54–55
    Loaded Sweet Potato Fries Board, 50–51
    Mediterranean Grazing Board, 38–39
    Netflix Night for Two Board, 36, 52–53
    Ombré Farmers' Market Board, 40–41
    Overnight Guest Welcome Board, 64–65
    Pantry Essentials Snack Board, 42–43
    Post-Workout Lunch Board, 62–63
    Stone Fruit Panzanella Salad Board, 44–45
    Vegan Banh Mi Board, 46–47
Grilled Cheese and Roasted Tomato Soup Board, 82–83

H

Hearty Pinto and Black Bean Chili, 68, 140
Hot Chocolate, Salted, 147
Hot Chocolate Dessert Board, 126–27
hummus, 14
    Roasted Beet Hummus, 132
    Roasted Red Pepper Hummus, 132

I

Ice Cream Sundae Board, 124–25
ingredient labels, 14
Instant Pot Vegan Oatmeal, 140

J

Jackfruit, Banh Mi Pulled, 135
Jam, Rustic Peach, with Thyme, 132–33

L

lemons
    Lemon Artichoke Dip, 140–41
    Lemon Blueberry Quinoa Muffins, 141
    Lemony Pea Pesto, 141–42
Lentil Balls, Cauliflower, 137
Loaded Sweet Potato Fries Board, 50–51
Loaded Vegan Chili Board, 68, 86–87

M

Mac and Cheese, Vegan, 134
Maple and Date Sweet Potato Dip, 142

meal boards, 13

    Build-Your-Own Sloppy Joes Board, 76–77

    Cincinnati-Style Chili Dinner Board, 78–79

    Coconut Chickpea Curry Board, 84–85

    Coconut Peanut Noodle Bowls Board, 70–71

    Grilled Cheese and Roasted Tomato Soup Board, 82–83

    Loaded Vegan Chili Board, 68, 86–87

    Rainbow Chopped Salad Board, 88–89

    Sunday Night Pasta Board, 74–75

    Taco Bowl Tuesday Board, 72–73

    Teriyaki Cabbage Wraps Board, 80–81

Mediterranean Grazing Board, 38–39

Melon Sparkler Board, Sweet and Spicy, 18, 28–29

Midsummer Backyard BBQ Board, 94–95

Mini Banana Bundt Cakes, 110, 142

Mini Berry Pie Board, 112–13

Mini Bundt Cakes Board, 110, 122–23

Mini Pie Crusts, 131

Miso Roasted Brussels Sprouts, 143

Muffins, Lemon Blueberry Quinoa, 141

mushrooms

    Chickpea Scramble with Mushrooms, 138

    Sautéed Mushrooms, 147

    Veggie Taco Crumbles, 150

N

Netflix Night for Two Board, 36, 52–53

New Year's Eve Champagne Toast Board, 90, 106–7

O

Oatmeal, Instant Pot Vegan, 140

Oatmeal Board, Grab-and-Go, 26–27

Oktoberfest Grazing Board, 98–99

Ombré Farmers' Market Board, 40–41

onions

    Caramelized Onion Dip, 136

    Quick Pickled Carrots or Red Onions, 145

Orange Vanilla Chia Pudding, 143

Overnight Guest Welcome Board, 64–65

P

packaged foods, 10, 13, 14

Pan con Tomate, 143

Pantry Essentials Snack Board, 42–43

Panzanella Salad Board, Stone Fruit, 44–45

Pasta Board, Sunday Night, 74–75

Peach Jam with Thyme, Rustic, 132–33

Peanut Noodle Sauce, Coconut, 131

Pea Pesto, Lemony, 141–42

Pie Crusts, Mini, 131

pie fillings

    Blueberry Chia Pie Filling, 133–34

    Strawberry Chia Pie Filling, 134

Pimentón Roasted Carrots, 144

Pistachio Cabbage Slaw, 144

Pizza Dough Garlic Knots, 144

Pizza Party Board, 108–9

Popcorn, Savory Dill, 147

Post-Workout Lunch Board, 62–63

potatoes

    Rosemary Mashed Potatoes, 146–47

    Spiced Potatoes and Cauliflower, 148

Pretzel Sparklers, Chocolate-Dipped, 130

Primal Kitchen sauces and condiments, 14

Pudding, Orange Vanilla Chia, 143

Pumpkin-Spiced Pumpkin Seeds, 145

Q

Quick Pickled Carrots or Red Onions, 145
quinoa
> Lemon Blueberry Quinoa Muffins, 141
> Quinoa Tabbouleh Salad, 131–32

R

Rainbow Chopped Salad Board, 88–89
Red Pepper Hummus, Roasted, 132
Red Sangria, 145
Red Wine Vinaigrette, 146
Roasted Beet Hummus, 132
Roasted Red Pepper Hummus, 132
Roasted Tomato Soup with Rosemary, 146
rosemary
> Roasted Tomato Soup with Rosemary, 146
> Rosemary Mashed Potatoes, 146–47
Rustic Peach Jam with Thyme, 132–33

S

salad dressings. *See* vinaigrettes
salads
> Chickpea Salad Sandwiches, 137
> Quinoa Tabbouleh Salad, 131–32
> Rainbow Chopped Salad Board, 88–89
> Stone Fruit Panzanella Salad Board, 44–45
Salted Hot Chocolate, 147
sandwiches
> Build-Your-Own Bagel Sandwich Board,
>   34–35
> Chickpea Salad Sandwiches, 137
> Vegan Grilled Cheese Sandwich, 150
Sangria, Red, 145
Sangria Board, Afternoon Tapas and, 48–49
sauces
> Classic Buffalo Sauce, 129
> Coconut Peanut Noodle Sauce, 131
> Sticky Sesame Garlic Sauce, 129
> Sweet and Spicy Adobo Sauce, 130
> Vegan Cheese Sauce, 134
> Vegan Chocolate Sauce, 149–50
Sautéed Mushrooms, 147
Savory Dill Popcorn, 147
seasonal and celebration boards
> Fall Harvest Board, 102–3
> Game Day Cauliflower Wings Board, 92–93
> Midsummer Backyard BBQ Board, 94–95
> New Year's Eve Champagne Toast Board, 90,
>   106–7
> Oktoberfest Grazing Board, 98–99
> Pizza Party Board, 108–9
> Spring Forward Board, 100–101
> Thanksgiving Snack Board, 96–97
Winter Solstice Board, 104–5
seeds. *See also* chia seeds
> Pumpkin-Spiced Pumpkin Seeds, 145
Sesame Garlic Sauce, Sticky, 129
Slaw, Pistachio Cabbage, 144
Sloppy Joes, Tempeh, 149
Sloppy Joes Board, Build-Your-Own, 76–77
soups
> Butternut Squash Soup Shooters, 136
> Roasted Tomato Soup with Rosemary, 146
Spiced Potatoes and Cauliflower, 148
Spring Forward Board, 100–101
Sticky Sesame Garlic Sauce, 129
Stone Fruit Panzanella Salad Board, 44–45
strawberries, 10
> Strawberry Cashew Cheesecake Dip, 133
> Strawberry Chia Pie Filling, 134
Sunday Night Pasta Board, 74–75
supplies, for building boards, 14–16
Sweet and Savory Toast Board, 22–23
Sweet and Spicy Adobo Sauce, 130
Sweet and Spicy Melon Sparkler Board, 18, 28–29

sweet potatoes
    Loaded Sweet Potato Fries Board, 50–51
    Maple and Date Sweet Potato Dip, 142
    Sweet Potato Breakfast Bowls Board, 32–33
    Sweet Potato Brownie Bowls, 36, 148
    Whipped Sweet Potato and Carrots, 151

T

Tabbouleh Salad, Quinoa, 131–32
Taco Bowl Tuesday Board, 72–73
Taco Crumbles, Veggie, 150
tempeh, 13
    BBQ Tempeh Burgers, 128
    Cincinnati-Style Vegan Chili, 130–31
    Tempeh Sloppy Joes, 149
Teriyaki Cabbage Wraps Board, 80–81
Thanksgiving Snack Board, 96–97
Toast Board, Sweet and Savory, 22–23
tomatoes
    Pan con Tomate, 143
    Roasted Tomato Soup with Rosemary, 146
Tortilla Bowls, Baked, 135

V

Vanilla Chia Pudding, Orange, 143
Vanilla Glaze, 143
Vegan Banh Mi Board, 46–47
vegan boards
    about, 10, 13
    building, 13–14
    supplies for, 14–16
Vegan Breakfast Burrito Board, 30–31
Vegan Cheese Board, Date Night, 58–59
vegan cheese products, 13
Vegan Cheese Sauce, 134
Vegan Chili, Cincinnati-Style, 130–31
Vegan Chili Board, Loaded, 68, 86–87

Vegan Chocolate Sauce, 149–50
Vegan Grilled Cheese Sandwich, 150
Vegan Mac and Cheese, 134
Vegan Oatmeal, Instant Pot, 140
Veggie Taco Crumbles, 150
vinaigrettes
    Basic Balsamic Vinaigrette, 135
    Red Wine Vinaigrette, 146

W

Waffle Bowls Board, Winter Yogurt, 120–21
Warm Arugula and Artichoke Dip, 150–51
Watermelon Pizza Board, 118–19
Whipped Sweet Potato and Carrots, 151
wine
    Red Sangria, 145
Winter Solstice Board, 104–5
Winter Yogurt Waffle Bowls Board, 120–21

Y

Yogurt Waffle Bowls Board, Winter, 120–21